Volum

MW00677335

DEEPERWOMEN™
TEACH

Stories and Strategies for Life, Love, and
Leadership from Women Who Lead

A Literary Collaborative by

Dr. Barbara Swinney

With Expert Authors

Lee Davis

Barbara Bond-Gentry

Dr. Rhonda Harris Thompson

Deidre Miller

Lesli Odum

Bree Reid

Dearice Spencer-Shackleford

Sandra Tescum

PUBLISHING COMPANY

4813 Ridge Road
Suite 111
Atlanta, Georgia

Copyright © 2024 by Dr. Barbara Swinney

First printing: April 2024

ISBN: 978-1-7325253-4-4

Printed in the United States of America

DEDICATION

For every woman who has ever come to the end of herself
and decided she wanted to become something different.

About the Brand

The DEEPER Women™ Brand was created in 2018 with the launch of Dr. Barbara Swinney's first book, "It's Always DEEPER: Six Steps to Achieving Perpetual Success"—the feature at the first DEEPER Women™ Conference, DEEPER Women™ Speak. This conference would establish the brand as a platform for women who lead to share their stories and strategies for life, love, and leadership. It would be the first in a series of DEEPER Women™ events and products. Since the launch, the brand, in collaboration with BSI Life and Leadership Consulting and BSI Publishing, has expanded to include the establishment of The DEEPER Leader Institute for Personal and Professional Development (an accredited coaching certification institute), the "Living the DEEPER Life" Companion Journal, the DEEPER Women™ Lead Annual Conference; and now, this Literary Collaborative-"DEEPER Women™ Teach: Stories and strategies for life, love, and leadership from women who lead."

CONTENTS

DEEPER WOMEN™ LEAD GLOBAL

Empowering women worldwide to heal, lead, and LEVERAGE their stories and strategies for life, love, and leadership.

INTRODUCTION

When I started this journey of wholeness and healing, I kept bumping into myself; I kept running into Barbara, but I did not recognize her because she looked like you. I had heard untold story after untold story, stories that could have unlocked my alabaster box twenty years ago—but nobody could step outside of themselves long enough to free me. I had heard stories of toxic relationships, mental, emotional, and spiritual suppression, illnesses caused by the stress of abuse, and the tragic outcomes of cyclical dysfunction. Sadly, most of the women I spoke with were telling their stories for the first time…to me! They had spent years going it alone, years of hopelessness and silent frustration. They had done the same thing I was guilty of doing—putting on the Red Ruby Woo Lipstick and heels and walking around confidently insecure, bound by the expectations of others, paralyzed by self-judgment, and completely afraid to give any indication that things were not OK.

That is why I became vigilant about helping women, like you, transition through life-changing events, while managing the demands of their roles as leaders. That is why this book is so important. DEEPER Women™ are real women, tackling real issues, leading in the real world, and living a real life.

This literary collaborative, written by eight powerful DEEPER Women™ who lead, is a collection of stories and strategies for life, love, and leadership to empower other women who lead! Get to know the authors through their stories and learn about how they experienced breakthroughs and breakouts; learn how you can heal and lead in your profession. To get the most out of this book, take notes and be intentional in implementing the tips and strategies provided to help you navigate life as it happens right in the middle of your leadership.

If You Want Your Life to Go Higher...

Go DEEPER!

Dr. Barbara Swinney

Everything I thought I would say, I did not. I anxiously waited to meet with my counselor to discuss the demise of my marriage. I had my tears on ready and my anger set to trigger; just waiting to let her eavesdrop on the conversation in my head; the inner banter about how I found out that my husband was living a double life for years and how within thirty days of our divorce, he was engaged. How was I supposed to help my girls navigate this dysfunction? How was I going to hide my grief from the people at work; the people I was charged with leading? The humiliation of it all—the pain and agony of realizing that the last twenty years of my life was an illusion, of sorts, was bewildering. The man that my girls and I greeted at the door upon his return from his "business trips", was really returning to us from his other life—one in which we did not exist. In this house of cards, she was the "wife". Who does this? The depth of the deception was mind boggling and left me questioning my identity, my judgment, and my intelligence. Reassuring myself, I continued to engage, "I know I'm smart; brilliant in fact". "I'm a good woman. Any man would love to have me love him. How did I miss this? Why did I allow myself to accept so little?"

The counselor entered the office. We exchanged pleasantries and then it was time, time for me to let her in on my diatribe! I opened my mouth, ready to spew it all, and NOTHING! None of the thoughts would form into words. At the very moment that I attempted to speak; I had a stunning revelation. Almost every sentence or question I posed during my mental babbling included the word "I" How did "I" miss this? "I" allowed...; "I" lost... It became clear that "I" was in the middle of it all. The anger and urge to blame dissipated. I became less interested in hating my ex and more concerned about my own healing. If I were going to *live* a full life for the rest of my life, I would have to take the steps necessary to mend my broken heart. I knew that if I wanted my life to go higher, I would have to go D-E-E-P-E-R!

This is exactly where the DEEPER Framework was established. While writing my first book, "It's Always DEEPER", I developed the framework to help readers get unstuck. As I began to heal, I found myself using the concept to help me navigate the healing process. I have included the Framework here for your reference as you continue to heal and lead on your journey to you.

Discover Your Purpose and Decide What You Want—

Clarify your vision and get clear about what you would like to accomplish.

Examine Your Life—

Identify behaviors that have impeded your progress. Figure out why you do what you do.

Eliminate the Barriers—

Replace negative behaviors with those that move you forward toward your goals and the life you want to live.

Plan of Action—

Determine the steps necessary to get what you want! Be specific and intentional in the action steps to accomplish your goals.

Evaluate Your Progress—

Get honest with yourself regarding your progress, celebrate, and adjust as necessary.

Realize That You Can Do It! —

Apply these principles in life and you WILL reach your goals and become who you want to be!

Discover Your Purpose and Decide What You Want—

While I learned about the long-term infidelity in my marriage, I also experienced a significant shift in my career as a leader in education. Twenty years into a career—with nothing less than exemplary ratings—I was literally tapped on the shoulder and told that my services were no longer needed in that position. Without explanation, I was technically demoted first in my marriage and then in my career. The two things with which I most readily identified were stripped away. This compounded the devastation. Who was I without them?

Somewhere on life's path, I had lost my way. My identity had become enmeshed with that of my marriage and my career, I simply lost track of Barbara. I had to get clear about who I was, who I wanted to become, and what I wanted. It was important to establish a new vision for myself. I started by ***deciding*** to assume 100% responsibility for my life. Nothing that happened to me was my fault, but it was certainly my responsibility. It was I, who accepted less than I deserved (at home and work), who ignored signs of emotional abandonment and infidelity, who did not hold my former partner accountable, who became overdependent on my career for validation, and who stayed in both relationships much longer than morally obligated. My behavior had not aligned with what I had envisioned for my life, but I had made no adjustments, other than hope and pray that he would change and that I would regain a similar leadership position. I did not honor myself. I gave too much power to other people, things, and ideals.

Deciding to take responsibility for my part of the demise of my marriage and the unraveling of my career, allowed me to determine a path forward. Getting a different result in my life started with *deciding* that I wanted something different.

Go DEEPER:

At times, we all get stuck in a relationship, career, or even in our beliefs —feeling like our life just isn't what we envisioned it to be. You give your all to other people, entities, or ideals; the real you become silenced by the noise that life creates. If you have lost your way or become a little foggy about what you really want, DECIDING that you want something different is a great place to start. Take the time to contemplate the question: "What is it that I really want?"

_____

_____

_____

_____

_____

_____

_____

_____

_____

_____

_____

_____

_____

_____

_____

_____

Examine Your Life—

This was probably the most difficult process of all. I really had to figure out why I was doing what I was doing. I had to *examine* behaviors that had me stuck in a relationship that was clearly leading to an inevitable end. I surrendered so much power and personal control in my marriage. I lost sight of who I was as an individual, how to make decisions for myself, and simply how to run my own life. A prime example of this was blindly allowing my husband to handle the finances. When I found myself having to manage it all, I would literally have panic attacks. What was this? I had to find the underlying cause of it.

I read a quote by Miles Monroe, "You don't start believing until you start doubting." So, I started questioning EVERYTHING about my life. Who am I? Is this a career in education what I am supposed to be doing? Was he the person I was supposed to marry? What am I passionate about? What brings me joy? Who is in my circle? I have found this to be a powerful technique for clarity. When I took the time to consider these questions, I discovered purpose in the pain of divorce and demotion.

As I started to examine my marriage, I found dependent behavior that started long before the marriage. I was so concerned about what people, including my former husband, thought of me. All my life had been spent pursuing something—a degree, a promotion, status, the big house with the wrought iron fence, the husband, two kids, and the dog! The perfect "looking" life. What was the root of this need to please or be perceived as perfectly packaged?

Growing up, the youngest of ten, was like having my own little entourage to support and cheer me on from the very beginning. I remember times when my brothers and sisters would literally have physical fights overtaking me, THE BABY, on a trip to a friend's house or showing me off to that someone special. My family openly celebrated my every milestone and constantly sent the "Midas Touch" message to me. When I started walking, they erupted with praises, "Yeah, the baby is walking!". When I said my first word, they cheered with "Yeah, the baby is talking!" Every milestone: *the baby's going to school; the baby is graduating, the baby got her doctorate; the baby got a promotion, was celebrated.* Seeing Barbara "do" big things just became an unspoken norm. My family simply loves me. Though they were genuine in their doting, the constant admiration left me addicted to the approval of others, on an endless search for external affirmation, and a closeted perfectionist. I found myself constantly needing people to affirm me; to tell me how well I did, how good I looked, or how much I inspired them to be better. I suffered from what I refer to as the pedestal syndrome—high on the pedestal is where people would automatically place me. I did not solicit this position, gave no indication that I wanted to be there, and struggled to keep my balance atop such a narrow surface.

This need for the praise and approval of others and the need to have things just perfectly established in me an overwhelming, negative belief. If no one was clapping, I felt that what I did or who I was just was not worthy for the stage. Though these were my private thoughts, they often showed up in my behavior and ultimately in my life choices. I had become so dependent on the value that other people assigned to me that I stayed in an unhealthy marriage, developed a toxic relationship with my career, and constantly found myself doing things that I did not want to do to please people whom I knew did not like me.

By *examining* my life and identifying the root cause of negative behaviors, I was able to regain custody of myself. I was able to take my power back from the perception of people and give it to purpose!

Go DEEPER:

For me, the addiction to external affirmation and validation kept me in a place far longer than it should have. What is it for you? What is keeping you tethered to a place where you no longer belong? Examine the patterns of behavior that may be impeding your progress. Take some time to sit with yourself and search for the origin of the behavior.

_____

_____

_____

_____

_____

_____

_____

_____

_____

_____

_____

_____

_____

_____

_____

_____

_____

_____

Eliminate the Barriers—

The process of examining my life helped me stop blaming people, other entities, or ideals and prompted me to fix my focus on myself. With this new awareness of the addiction to external affirmation, I needed to break the addiction and adopt a new behavior. I had to establish, what I like to call, "replacement thought or replacement behavior". When I would feel the need to please or the urge to hold on to something, I would ask myself a few questions: What am I feeling? Where is this coming from? Is this a feeling or is it a fact? Why am I holding on to this? How is it serving me?

Taking just a few minutes to consider these questions completely shifted how I approached life, but more specifically, how I addressed life-changing events. As a part of the divorce, I had to sell the marital property and purchase a new home. I loved our family home; at least that is what I told myself. When I asked myself the question, "How does it serve me?" I was blown away by my response. The house no longer served me. I did not need it in the same way that I did—when it was purchased as marital property and a place to raise our children. The truth was, at approximately 5600 square feet, located in a premier community, the house represented status for me. I liked what it represented at the time of purchase and how it looked to other people. The other truth was that we were drowning in debt trying to keep up with the mortgage and the appearance. So, when it was time for me to purchase a new home, I was determined to begin living below my means, rid myself of debt, become financially secure, and live and model the life I wanted for myself. I was determined not to relapse!

Go DEEPER:

Consider some of the negative thought patterns or behaviors you uncovered while you were *examining* your life. What are you doing to change the pattern? What replacement thoughts or behaviors have you adopted and used regularly?

_____

_____

_____

_____

_____

_____

_____

_____

_____

_____

_____

_____

_____

_____

_____

_____

_____

_____

_____

_____

_____

_____

Plan Specific Action Steps—

I found many women just like me on this path. Many of them did not have the emotional tools or resources to deal with their grief in a way that was productive. I often found myself sharing my story of breaking down and my moments of breaking through. Seeing themselves reflected in my situation brought them hope; seeing myself in them gave me peace.

I knew that it was a part of my purpose to help other women walk boldly, brilliantly, and beautifully in their own purpose. It was essential to create the space to breathe, think, write, speak, and focus on my health so that I could be "available" for them. With the distractions of the divorce and shifts in my career, I knew I would need support to stay focused on my goals. I put my leadership skills to work and put together my team. I began seeing a therapist to help me manage my emotions and support my daughters. I hired a realtor who was responsible for the sale of the marital property and getting me into my new home. I learned the value of FaceTime to keep the lines of communication open with my college freshman. I hired a mentor to help me with my new business and got myself a writing coach!

I literally cleared an area in my home and claimed it as "MINE" …and marked it as such. I committed to writing my first book. I bought a special journal specifically for this process. In it, I included a weekly schedule of days and times that I would dedicate to writing, a section for goal setting, and a place to record weekly assessments of my progress. My writing coach provided guidance and helped me to grow and develop as a writer.

Go DEEPER:

Perhaps you are thinking, *I can't afford to hire all those people or who could not reach their goals with all those resources?* Trust me, when you decide what you want, you gain clarity of vision. Once you are clear, there is very little that can stop you! Once you start acting on your vision, you will get creative about how to acquire the resources. Start with writing down what you have decided. Start by asking yourself these questions: *What do I need to get started? Whom do I know that can help me? What resources do I already have to get what I want?*

_____

_____

_____

_____

_____

_____

_____

_____

_____

_____

_____

_____

_____

_____

_____

_____

_____

_____

_____

_____

*E*valuate Your Progress—

I did the work! I decided, examined, eliminated, established a plan of action, and now…*How's that working for you?* I wanted to stay on track and needed to be intentional about evaluating my progress along the way. If I was going to create the conditions for perpetual success, I had to adopt a system that would answer that question. I needed a systematic way to **evaluate** my progress along the way. As I worked to find the most effective way to monitor and adjust my action steps, I began to examine some of my current practices in my role as a leader and life coach. There were certain processes that I used unconsciously, and I thought starting there would give me a clue as to how to evaluate and monitor my personal progress. I needed something simple; easy to use and readily applicable. I started paying close attention to how I did everything: from cleaning my house, to processes that I would follow at work, and practices that I would use to get results with my coaching clients. I ended up with this simple, four-step process that I used every week when I sat down to evaluate the progress toward my goals.

> **Step 1: REVIEW**—I knew that I wanted to use my story, my gift to help others see things differently, and my story to support women in leadership navigate life-changing events as they happened right in the middle of their leadership.

> **Step 2: REFLECT**—One of my goals was to tell my story to free other women. I decided to share my story in a book. As a part of my healing process, I started journaling my thoughts for the purpose of turning it into a book. I made sure I made time to write at least 30 minutes a day to accomplish this goal. Each

week, I would reflect on the goals to ensure that my actions were aligned.

Step 3: REVISE or REPLACE—when I assessed my writing progress if I found that I was not meeting my weekly writing goals, I would examine my actions to see what behaviors were impeding my progress.

Step 4: REPEAT—this is a process that I followed and continue to follow as a part of my practice to achieve perpetual success.

The weekly *evaluation* of my goals and actions really worked to keep me on target. No matter what I found when I looked back, I was always pleased because I knew exactly what I needed to do to regroup and reengage in the process. My goal was to write to inspire. No matter what your goal is, an intentional evaluation process is essential not only in your goal setting but in your supportive actions and strategies as well. You must develop a systematic way of evaluating your progress. Be intentional!

Go DEEPER:

Think about what you want for your life. What is your vision? What goals and action steps have you established to get what you want? Are your behaviors aligned with your vision and goals? What adjustments do you need to make?

_____

_____

_____

_____

_____

_____

_____

_____

_____

_____

_____

_____

_____

_____

_____

_____

_____

_____

_____

_____

_____

*R*ealize That You Can Do It! —

The divorce and the demotion have proven to be the most painfully rewarding experiences I have had. They provided the outside pressure I needed to begin examining what was really happening on the inside. The brokenness helped me to put the pieces back together in the way they were designed to fit.

After consistently and intentionally applying these strategies, I have been able to reach my goals and begin creating the life that I want. As you may have read in my bio, in a period of six months, I was divorced and demoted, bought a house, sold my marital home, sent a child off to college, and started a life and leadership coaching business to help women in leadership transition through life-changing events that occur right in the middle of their leadership!

I am not sure where you are right now. I do not know the struggles you are facing or what is keeping you from living the life you want. What I do know is that anything that you imagine for yourself is microscopic compared to your true capacity for "becoming". You have always had the power!

Go DEEPER:

Sometimes we get so lost in doing the work that we do not recognize that we have already done the work. Be careful to celebrate your successes. Take time to reflect during your daily quiet time. Keep a record of the things you are accomplishing. Honor yourself by celebrating who you are and what you have done. ***Realize that*** you can do it!

My name is Dr. Barbara Swinney…and I am Iyanla Vanzant; I am Michelle Obama; I am Oprah Winfrey; I am Yolanda, Becky, and Lisa…I am You!

The Joy and Pain in Rediscovering Me

Lee Davis

One minute, I was cracking jokes with my husband and kids, making plans for business expansion, and celebrating our daughters' new business that went viral; the next minute, I am sitting in the middle of my unkempt backyard, in a hard white plastic chair, surrounded by dry tumbleweeds. In total silence, inside of my empty thoughts; clueless of how I would get out of this predicament. All I had left in me to do was to talk to God. What happened? How did I get here? How did my life get so off track like this?

In my pillow talk with my husband, who will become my eh-husband, we discussed what we could contribute to our children and what beneficial attributes and skill sets do we hold inside to ensure our children are taught? My ex-husband is very skilled, highly intelligent, and skillful with his hands. However, he lacked patience and was often driven to exceed his abilities. This always triggered me. I never understood how anyone could settle with the cards they were provided with versus trying to build their deck of cards with the skill set they were blessed with. The conversation would go a little something like this. "What skill set are you leaving for the boys if you leave this earth?" He would respond, "They don't want to learn my skill set, and I am not going to force them to know it. If they want it, they will come get it. ""ell, what skill set"are you leaving the girls?" He asked. My reply was, ""or one! I am teachi"g them how to be a lady, how to pursue their goals and dreams, and always be able to financially care for themselves so that nobody will ever be able to control them with money." His reply, "Well, I don't see that as a skill set. I don't see you teaching them about business because all you do is read books and try to make a business out of something." He was right, and something about that statement was almost like a challenge to me. I am unsure if it was his sarcastic tone or the fact that he was speaking. He went on to say, "So, the fact is neither one of us is teaching our kids our skill sets, so leave me the hell alone about it". I had no clue what it was about that statement, but it triggered me. It triggered me badly.

Over the next few months, the girls were having a grand opening for their beauty supply store, and I was teaching them everything I could about owning and operating a business. As a family, we were right there supporting and cheering them on as their story went viral. They were being honored for being the youngest African American woman to own and operate a beauty supply store in the United States. In March 2016, they were a viral success. The girls were interviewed on Magic Johnson's 32 under 32, Essence, BET, Roots, and so many more outlets. The publicity seemed promising. However, although they had the publicity, they had no financial success. The business needed help. The girls, aged

18 and 21, were feeling the pressure of running and operating a business. They set out to please the outside world of the African American community and have a social life. I was so excited about where this business could go and how well it was being received. I became so consumed with success that I forgot to be a mother, and I forgot to be a wife.

I invested all my time in the "girls" shop, my 9-5, and my start-up nonprofit entrepreneurship program. I worked my 9-5, left work, went to the shop, and finished the night working my nonprofit, creating training material and anything else I needed to complete. At home, I was on computers, completing invoices, doing business consulting, and constantly focused on creating a life, or so I thought. My problems in the marriage hit its head. We weren't on solid terms to begin with, and if I am being honest, I would rather spend time creating a business than arguing with him or sitting idle in awkward silence next to him. In my opinion, he never saw me anyhow. It felt like a business partnership rather than a marriage. We paid bills together, took care of all the household business, and raised the kids. Consequently, in May 2017, on a day like any other, we went to dinner and mutually and cordially agreed to split.

My First Wake-Up Alarm: I Hit Snooze

Accepting other people's emotions and feelings are valid even if you do not understand them. One of my daughters struggled in the beauty supply industry because he never cared too much for it; her passion was art. Both girls also struggled with being in the public's eye with they didn't know calling their names out loud. They struggled with not having the finances they thought they would have by being in business. One of them became so overwhelmed by the public pressure to succeed and by pressure from me, her own mother. You always want your child to do well and keep going despite your feelings and emotions, but she struggled emotionally and mentally. She struggled with her own will and desire to leave the business altogether, knowing this would be disappointing to me, along with the feeling of letting the black community down that she contemplated suicide.

One day while I was at work, one of my daughters called to say I needed to come to the shop. Her sister was not doing well, and she felt her sister was going to hurt herself. One of my daughters has struggled with mental illness since the age of 13. I never accepted that as a fact and thought she was just a sensitive soul that I needed to take precautions with and be aware of my words and actions when dealing with her, which I admit I failed miserably short. For years, I couldn't relate to the fact that my daughter's mental illness surrounded her with suicidal tendencies. I didn't understand it. In my mind, I was carrying all her burdens and meeting her needs. I went to bat for her and on her behalf with school and everything else in life she attempted. What could stress her out so much that she would want to end her life? I was so naïve and, to be honest, in denial about the mental illness attached to my child. I simply didn't take it seriously. I had this mindset, "Girl, if I can do XYZ all these years and carry the burden on my own for all these years, you can handle a little stress." But this day was different.

I left work and headed straight to the girl's shop. When I arrived, my daughter was in front of the store. Her eyes looked sad, and I didn't even think we spoke; I just caught my eyes and walked directly to the back of the store. I opened the back door, and there she was, her eyes puffy and red and crying uncontrollably. For the first time, I was riddled with guilt because I not only saw her pain and dismay, but I felt it. For the first time, I wasn't momma the warden coming in with 100 questions on what's wrong and just doing this or that. I just wanted to be her mom at that moment. So, I didn't say one word, because no words were needed. I just held her tight and felt relief come over her. She hugged me and let out the most enormous, uncontrollable cry that made me cry. I just hugged my baby at that moment. I knew whatever was tormenting my daughter needed to stop by any means necessary. Once the tears subsided, I told her that if this business is making you feel like this, you need to walk away. Baby, walk away. There is nothing in life worth working for or working in that stresses you to the point where you feel this is the end. I told her that her happiness and her peace are what matters.

My daughter never worked again in the shop after that day. She relocated to Las Vegas, leaving the business to her sister to operate, and run. I was going through a divorce from their father, and although we agreed to continue to support the girls financially, that agreement didn't last even one month after the divorce. One daughter left the business, and the other began working part-time at a retail store, reducing the hours the store would open. Eventually, that daughter called it quits and moved to Vegas, leaving the store for her brother and me to run. Unfortunately, a few months later, we closed the shop completely because I worked a full-time job, and her brother was still in high school. The store would only operate after 3:30 pm and at weekends and wasn't bringing in enough money to maintain it any longer.

I learned about emotions during this time. Everyone handles their feelings and stress differently, and my job is to allow everyone to feel their way into and through their own emotions. What seemed so minor to me was revealed when I saw my daughter break down in the back of her business that day. What she felt and the immense pressure she felt under were genuine and real to her. Her view of the viral business, social media waves, and random strangers calling was different from mine. I viewed it as free marketing, publicity, and foot traffic. Everything was business in my eyesight. I needed to understand and show empathy for the stress that publicity brings when it is unsolicited and unwanted. I learned it was my dream to be a successful businessperson, not my daughter's dream. I was excited because they were experiencing something I had always wanted in business, but I lost track of the fact that this was not their dream but mine, and it humbled me. Due to that realization, my responsibility was to close the shop down.

My Second Wake-Up Alarm…Still Hitting Snooze

Emotional and financial stress. My parents, my son, and I cleared the store out. With limited financial resources and limited help, our only solution was to store all items at home. My home became a storage unit in the garage, and in the front half of my home, beauty supply equipment and inventory greeted me every day. Within eight months after my divorce, the store was closed, my daughters had moved away, and this 5-bedroom, 4-bathroom home now only had two occupants in it, and I was struggling to keep this big baby afloat. My savings were gone, and I felt all options were utterly obsolete. I have always been a very private person about my life with family and friends. I sincerely believe that people only care to listen when you are doing badly. So, I kept my bad and some of my good to myself.

When I was married to my ex-husband, we financially supported my mother and father after my mother's cancer led to my father's early retirement. Well, her cancer treatments were pre-Obama Care, so she was denied several times for insurance, and her entire treatment was out of pocket, which wiped away my parents' savings. They had to refinance their home to cover payments, which'caused the new mortgage to be too much for them, so they also lost their home. It was never an issue for my ex-husband and me to pitch in when needed, so we did this monthly. My parents were never the type to ask for help, and they helped so many people throughout the years that it was an honor to give back to them. We did this monthly for a few years. But I wasn't honest with them about my financial situation when I divorced. All they knew was that the girls gave up on the shop and moved to Vegas. They didn't realize the severity of my financial hardship.

My mother called to ask if I had any money for them to get some groceries. I couldn't keep up with providing for them in the hardship I faced. The ego is a deadly disease. I was too prideful, to be honest, and tell my mother my situation because I didn't want to tell her, and two, I didn't want her to stress over me, and she had her own needs. I was going to figure it out in some form or fashion. After telling her for the first time, I am sorry, Mom. I don't have anything to give you guys but hold on, let me figure it out. My mom says, Oh no, oh no, don't worry about it, that's fine. I got off the phone and had a total meltdown with my siblings.

I called my oldest sister and brother and just went on a full-blown yelling tantrum. I expressed everything I had been hiding and what I had been dealing with financially. I didn't care about whatever judgment, as they would let loose on me. I just let it all out, telling them how I felt and how they should step up and help. I've been taking care of Mom and Dad for years now. It is your turn. You all need to step up and help! I can't do it anymore! To my surprise, they bo'h just listened, didn't argue, and didn't throw stones; they listened, and my sister said, "Lee, you are correct; it is our turn now," and she spoke. "I got them". It is truly amazing how God will shift situations and people and place them in the season they should be. Because when I was face down struggling, my sister's finances were upward, and she stepped right in where I left off and began assisting our parents. Later, that role shifted, and my brother stepped up and took his turn helping my parents until their finances finally shifted to where they could be self-sufficient once again. My parents being ok was a sigh of relief, a moment to focus on getting myself out of my hole.

I had tried for months to get my ex-husband to sign divorce papers so that I could remodify my mortgage to make it more manageable for me. My ex-husband dodged the signature of the documents for months; in the process, my savings were depleted on my mortgage and the expenses at my daughter's beauty supply shop until it closed. I was completely tapped out financially and mentally.

My finances had become so depleted that I wouldn't have gas to make it to work on some days, and I began calling out of work due to not having gas to get there. Eventually, my son and I began putting inventory on the offer-up app and other sites to try to sell equipment and beauty supply inventory. I started taking products such as hair oils, wigs, braiding hair, eyelashes, and anything I could to my job and selling items out of my car to coworkers. I would leave in the morning with just enough gas to make it to work and with prayers to sell the items to get me just enough money to make it home. The financial stress was so overwhelming it saturated my thoughts day and night. How can I get out of this situation?

I was trying everything to make ends meet. Selling beauty supply products at the job to make ends meet at home, I am still providing business consulting to startup businesses and picking up a little cash here and there to pay bills and other things for the household. But my son and I were still struggling, and I was getting frustrated. I was still working on my entrepreneurship training material and finally had my first real break. I met with the local school district, and they wanted my program at the school and referred me to my local City Mayor and City Manager to discuss funding. After speaking with all parties involved, I was given the government Small Business Administration contact information. This was my golden ticket, guys. The small business administration contractor connects me with his local agency for the Small Business Development Center Inland Empire. They fund them, and they are supposed to provide funding to other programs in my area, such as mine, and this turns out to be one of my biggest nightmares ever!

Just rip the pages out now! Say it with me now: long story short, the Small Business Development Center Inland Empire "stole" my training material and began teaching it locally as their program on How to start a small business. I am livid! How do I know they did this? They posted it on Facebook after our meeting, stating that our new entrepreneurship training program is coming soon. They provided a date that they would host their first class, and I signed up for it only to see my PowerPoint materials being shared as their material, and I called out the presenter. The guy I met in person to discuss my program. I was crushed, like how the government steals your work. I wasn't sure if I should be flattered like oh wow, the government thought my training materials were so good that they had to take it for their material. Or should I be insulted that they dismissed me and felt they could take it just because I am a nobody? Who's going to believe the federal government took Lee's training material? This was my big break, and now it's gone. I don't have any money to hire an attorney, so what do I do? Do I sue? Let's just say I will release this information as part two.

But, before I can even get settled with realizing my golden ticket training material is gone and prepare to fight for it, I get a call from my daughter in Las Vegas. My daughter is telling me her sister, my other daughter, is having a mental breakdown, and she needs my help to calm her down. Emotions overload, right? Now, I must shift from upset fighter mode to change my hat back to mother bear mode and nurture my daughter. I relax and get on the phone to talk to my daughter. It took me almost 4 hours to get her on the phone. I don't know how to explain to people when you have a child with suicidal tendencies, every distress telephone call you get, your heart stops; every time that child isolates himself and refuses to communicate, your heart stops. I don't care how strong and how independent and how much psychology you have under your belt when the phone rings and you hear a distressed voice from someone regarding your child, a million thoughts cross your mind, and none of them are positive until you hear that child's voice, or you see that child's face. I reach her, speak with her, calm her down, and pray with her. I express my absolute love and admiration for her. She opened up and let me know when she wanted to end her life, she heard a voice say, "Your mother would never recover." She said she stopped and thought of me, and I cried and told her that her voice was correct. I thanked her for loving me so much; she thought of me over herself, and I expressed my love for her.

The Breaking Point

My daughter is aware of her struggles and admits it is a constant mental battle. Ironically, she couldn't relate to how her siblings felt or how her mother felt every time we received a phone call regarding her distress. Every time thinking, "Is this the final call today"? Not even 30 days after her meltdown in Las Vegas, I had to call her and her sister to tell them about the fear I had just gone through with their brother.

My sister and brother came to town, and we hadn't been together in a celebratory manner for some years. I think my telephone call shook them a while back, so they just wanted to come out and check on me. We hung out at my home and were having a fantastic evening until about midnight; I received a distress call from my son's friend stating he was trying to jump off a freeway overpass. This blew my mind. I said, "My son, my son"!. His friend said. "Yes, Ms. Lee". I charged him and stopped him, but he took off running. My whole thoughts 'ere like, what in the world is going on? Why would he be trying to hur' himself? So, my sister and I jumped into the car and drove the streets looking for him. We drove for hours to the point my stomach was in knots. I told my sister to stop the car and take me home. She kept saying no, let's try this street or this area. I yelled to her, "No, stop the car and take me home"! I yelled,

"Either my son is going to have to be strong enough to fight his demons, or I am going to have to be strong enough to bury my son! Take me home"! That was the most enlightening, heart-wrenching moment of my life. The realization that I cannot protect my kids, I cannot stop them from hurting themselves, I cannot be everywhere at one time, I cannot do anything to prevent or stop anything. I cannot control their actions. I was powerless yet so awakened in that moment.

But when I tell you when it's your wake-up call, if you keep hitting snooze, you will finally be shaken out of your bed and forced to do the work internally. I have a soft heart for my parents and my kids. I just need them to be cared for, which stresses me out if they are not. So now that I know my parents and kids will be okay, I have released them to God and pray over their mental, emotional, and financial strengths. My entire life, I have been someone else's problem solver. I am the fixer. But who fixes the fixer when the fixer can no longer operate?

The following day, I sat in my unkept backyard mid-morning in a hard white plastic chair surrounded by dry tumbleweed. I was sitting in total silence, just my blank thoughts, and I was clueless on how I would get out of this financial predicament and why my kids were being attacked with suicidal thoughts. I instantly knew it was an attack spiritually. Nothing made sense, and too many things were going haywire at once. It was as if I was being tested to be broken down on all levels. The finances were a struggle, but finances never defined me. I knew that would be temporary. I just needed my one break, and I would be okay again financially. This is why I felt the target was on my kids because my kids are my weak spot, and if that attack on my kids could get me to fold and fall into a pit of despair, then that would have been a successful attack. As I sat in this chair, all these thoughts surrounded me. I talked to God harder than I ever did before. I spoke to him as if he was right next to me. The more I spoke, the stronger my voice became; the more I spoke, I could feel the authority rise in me, the confidence, the belief, and the knowing that I was protected, my kids were protected, and no weapon formed against me would prosper. My life shifted at that moment.

The following week, October 4, 2018, I received my pay, paid my mortgage and a couple bills. After paying those few bills, I had only four dollars left. I was only paid once a month so that was it for guaranteed income. I knew I had to get creative because I had to be at work that following Monday, and my tank was empty. My son and I scrambled around the house searching for more money to add to those four dollars. We found two dollars and some change. On Monday, I gathered the beauty supply products, put my six dollars in the tank, and went to work.

That week was an odd one; I will never forget it. Every day that week, I would leave home to head to work with my car on empty and sell a product to get back home. Stressful, you would think. Every day that week, I would take my break and take a walk. I felt light, unbothered, and at ease. The colors on my walk seemed brighter. I could hear the birds soothing my spirit. They were chirping and singing as if they were serenading me. There was absolutely no reason for me to be so light and happy, but I was. I can't describe it, but I felt God's presence with me every day that week. Someone would buy a product every day, and it would be enough to get home and back the next day. God's grace surrounded me because my tank would be on empty when I left my home, yet somehow God got me all over the city.

I spoke with my daughters in Las Vegas. My daughter who was working told me she gets paid on Thursday and will send us some money. I recall simply saying, okay, baby. My daughter called me Thursday and said something happened to her check. They made an error and told her they would fix it by Friday. I said, "It's okay, baby, someone purchased something. I have enough to get home". Friday came, and oddly, not one soul purchased anything. My daughter calls and says, "My job is tripping; they still haven't fixed my check, and I haven't gotten paid yet." Then she asked me, "Did anyone buy anything today?" I replied honestly, "No, not today". My daughter started panicking. "Oh, Lord, Mom, just ask someone if you can borrow some gas money." My daughter says this knowing I don't borrow money. I told her I would be fine, and I said, "Girl, God got me."

I get off work at 3:30 pm, and I am usually shutting down my computer and heading out the door at that time, but that day, I had no money or gas to get home from work, so I just sat there. I don't know why. I guess I was just thinking. That's when I heard him say, "Check your account." I laughed to myself. I already knew nothing was in that account, so I initially ignored that voice. Then the voice got extremely loud, almost like, "Are you mocking me?" "CHECK YOUR ACCOUNT!" It was so forceful that it made me sit up and log into my account. I couldn't believe it. I had $19.10 cents in my account. I sat back in my chair, looked up towards God, and shook my finger as I nodded. Someone had ordered inventory online from our online store which no one had ever ordered from before. I called my son and asked him to confirm the products were available. He said, "Yes, they are. Why?" I said, "We just got an online order and need to ship them to the customer immediately. I smiled and thanked God the whole way home. I had to be on cloud 9. I was so excited because I knew exactly where that money came from. I knew he carried me and tested my faith all week. It gave me just enough to get home and back for a week. I could have easily become frustrated, stressed out, and complained, but I was high on God that whole week without even knowing the blessing he had in store for me.

I Am Up Now!

God shows up and shows out to his faithful ones. I arrived at my home after worshiping God the whole trip home. My son didn't even allow me to exit the car. He swung the front door open, saying, Mom, what is going on? People have been hitting us up on Offer Up, and this guy just came and purchased the open sign for fifty dollars. My son and I were dancing by the front door. I know the neighbors were probably thinking we were crazy, but my Lord. That fifty dollars felt good. I logged into Offer Up, and we had two inquiries about the products. The first lady wanted to come by and see what we had that day. She arrived about an hour later and spent 500.00 dollars. When she left, we had a full-blown dance- off in the house. Another lady, who was in the process of opening her own beauty supply store, came by and wanted a price for EVERYTHING. I wanted to be a blessing to her like she was being a blessing to me. I know she felt like we were her angels, but she was truly ours. So, we sold her everything for five thousand dollars.

We started October 2018, with four dollars and within seven days we had 5500.00, and since that day my account hasn't been in the negative. Nothing changed for me financially from 2018 until 2020, but

I changed. So, I say to you, "Stay faithful, stay positive, stay encouraged! When God shows up to show you his favor, He doesn't just sprinkle you with blessings. He pours them down over and around you".

Mindset Shift: Abundance Begins to Flow

In January 2020, while at work, I noticed so many people getting sick. It began on one side of the office, and every day, it seemed as if it was coming closer and closer to my side. An emergency announcement came out informing all of us to stay home if we felt ill. Before long, the entire staff was coughing, and this illness completely took over the office and spread throughout the whole building. I recall speaking with another coworker who was so ill he was at his desk shaking with a blanket. I had worked with him for almost ten years, and this guy never missed work. He said, "Lee, I have never felt like this."

In March 2020, a major announcement came out: "Unlimited overtime! Effective immediately!" The world was in a pandemic, and my job was considered essential. Office memos came out stating that if you have preexisting health conditions or lived with someone who has health concerns, please inform your manager so you can work from home. We begin to see staff grabbing computers and leaving to work from home. My turn came, and I gathered my belongings and was sent to work from home. The second shocking memo came out announcing there will be unlimited overtime from 6:00 am to 8:00 pm 7 days a week until further notice with no limitations. If you can work, overtime is approved. It was the craziest, most unheard-of thing ever. Many of my coworkers began to speculate that they would give us until the end of the year so let's enjoy this moment and get this money.

I was in complete awe. Here I am, struggling to get gas money to make it to work, and now there's no need to worry about gas. I am working from home and can work as much overtime as possible. While the presence of as pandemic was tumultuous and upsetting. My mindset was, "God is shifting circumstances in my favor." That statement continuously played in my mind. This was my opportunity to get out of debt, and maybe, just maybe, I could get enough to fix my home up the way I had imagined over the years.

My plan was to work as much as possible to get some breathing room. Although many of my coworkers complained that they had to work so many hours to bring home a decent amount and others just sat home and received free government money, I just felt like I prayed for help, and God answered. He didn't say, "Okay, let me give you the finances you need. God said, "Let me see how badly you need or want it." He said, "This is the door of opportunity. Do you take it or complain? You must work for it and not compare your situation to others. So, let me tell you something. I know a blessing when I see one. I didn't care if I had to work my fingers to the bone. The opportunity was there, and I was going to seize it.

Over nine months, I worked every day from 6 am until 8 pm for seven days a week. In 2021, I slowed down, reduced my hours, and began taking vacations. Yes, during the pandemic, I had my best vacation ever. I was not only able to get myself out of debt and get a good cushion of savings under me, but I was also able to help my parents and my kids, during this time. I was able to renovate my entire home and travel the world to visit places such as Ghana and Egypt in Africa, to name a few. This time, although painful to many, was a relief for me. I felt a little guilty, but it was the best time of my life. I worked my tail off, and the rewards and the benefits I received were nothing short of amazing. God's grace and abundance surrounded me. I went from struggling to pay my mortgage two years earlier to purchasing my second home and starting a recovery business. All I was concerned about was doing right by God, paying off my bills, sowing a seed into others, and staying humble amid abundance and uncertainty.

I was never one to ask for help; working for what I wanted gave me so much joy. I never paid attention to who was watching me or who spoke about me, whether positive or negative. My prayer was always to be blessed and be a blessing to others. I returned to my entrepreneurship job and began counseling and mentoring individuals in business start-ups for free. That was my gift, so I began to give back. I created a vision board in 2018 but saw little in 2019, so I created another one.

In 2020, almost everything on my vision board from 2018 had come to pass. It blew my mind. I was truly living a life of manifestation without even knowing I was actively manifesting my goals into reality. That dark time in my life, when I sat in a white outdoor plastic chair in the middle of a dry backyard, was one of the lowest points of life but the most empowering time. I had to sit in silence in my solitude with my thoughts. I had no clue what my life would look like, where I was going, or how to get there. But I knew sitting there crying and thinking of everything going wrong was not the answer. I always say solitude is where lonely hearts go to repair themselves.

Go DEEPER!

"God is shifting people, places, and circumstances in my favor"

– author unknown.

This was my "go-to" quote: allowing me to push through when I felt all odds were against me. I knew if it were meant to happen in my favor— God would align the shifts necessary for my success.

Find the meaning in you without attaching yourself to anyone or anything else. Stay focused on you. To get to the best version of yourself, you must begin working on it.

Be blessed and be a blessing.

Bounce Back:

From the Bottom to the Boss

Barbara Bond-Gentry

"Get it together, Bee, you got this!" I kept telling myself, but truth be told, I had everything but 'this'! I had sweaty palms, my legs trembled, and my mouth was as dry as the desert, but the one thing I did not have was 'this'. I was struggling miserably; panic set in as I prepared to take the stage, yet I could barely feel my feet. Nothing was working. I had prepared for this moment. This was my big shot, my time to shine. I had all of my notes, yet somehow, I became so paralyzed with fear that I couldn't remember my name, the mission statement, the target audience, or any other part of the carefully crafted message my coach had asked me to deliver. I remember looking at the clock and thinking we might run out of time, and I'll have another day to get myself together. Then, with a sinking heart, I heard the announcement: "Next up to the stage, BARBARA BOND-GENTRY! "

Summoning just enough courage, I took the stage. Gripping the mic, I scanned the audience and froze. What was happening? I had delivered countless speeches before this moment. I am an ordained evangelist, for goodness' sake. I'd stood before thousands to declare the word of God, but now, in front of ten like-minded successful women and my millionaire coach, I had nothing. My mind went completely blank. For the first time in my life, I was speechless.

My coach saw that I was struggling and quickly joined me onstage. A sense of relief came over me because I thought for sure she was going to save me! Surprisingly, she only asked me one question, which had nothing to do with my vision, mission, or target audience. She asked me: "Who told you that you weren't good enough, and when did you start believing it."

My eyes immediately began to fill with tears; memories that I hadn't thought about in years started to flood my mind, and I found myself feeling more exposed than ever. I didn't know how to respond. Do I speak, cry, or remain silent? All I wanted to do was run off that stage, find the nearest exit, and never look back. Instead, I blurted out "my former boss"! She looked me straight in my eyes and said, no, go back further than that. She urged me to confront the roots of my insecurity. In other words, she challenged me to go DEEPER.

Facing Your Past

Out of nowhere, a memory resurfaced from my childhood that I had suppressed entirely. I received straight A's on my report card in the sixth grade. I could hardly wait for the school day to end because I was so excited to get home and show everybody what I had done! Indeed, they would celebrate this accomplishment and be so proud of me. I was always an excellent student, yet my achievements were seldom acknowledged. But this time felt different. This was perfection, a milestone I had never reached. In my mind, I could hear the cheers and celebration that awaited. I busted through the doors and screamed, look, everybody; I got all A's! My grandmother started to say that's great, Barbara, but before she could finish her sentence, someone screamed, "Oh, that's nothing; you are in elementary school; just wait until you get to middle and high school; you will never do that again." Instantly, I felt stripped of value and left questioning my worth.

Clutching my report card, I ran back outside and sat on the porch. I couldn't believe it. My best was still not good enough. I remember thinking, what's so wrong with me that I'm not worth celebrating? The rejection stung, leaving me grappling with feelings of inadequacy and self-doubt. Yet as swiftly as despair settled in, so did the distraction of my friends from up the street, prompting me to cast aside my disappointment, discard my report card, and join them in playing games. Unbeknownst to me then, those fleeting moments of rejection would leave a lasting imprint on my life, shaping my self-perception for years to come.

As I began to connect the dots, I saw how those childhood feelings of inadequacy echoed in my adult struggles. But why did they resurface now, stealing the spotlight on this pivotal moment? And more importantly, how could I banish them and reclaim this stage?

Unfazed by my emotional turmoil, my coach pressed on, urging me to revisit every instance where those feelings had shaped my actions. Defensive walls rose within me, but she persisted, refusing to let my reluctance hinder her mission. I could almost hear her urging me to confront those buried emotions, acknowledge them, and ultimately release them.

Suddenly, in front of total strangers, I relived some of my life's most challenging experiences. Emotions and memories I had guarded closely, never daring to share with another soul, spilled forth openly in the presence of these successful women. I knew I had come to a place within myself where the longing to be free and healed outweighed the urge to remain guarded and concealed—each of those moments stemmed from a shared source of childhood trauma. It became evident that the wounds inflicted on the young 6th-grade girl had never truly healed. She had only found ways to ensure she would never feel those feelings again by resorting to tactics like overcompensating while simultaneously downplaying her true capabilities. She often played small so that no one else would get the chance to minimize her best efforts. Despite being perceived as highly successful by others; she knew deep within herself that she had never truly showcased her full potential. But enough was enough! I decided then that I was worth fighting for.

So, the real work began, but here's the irony in that statement. I believed the work had already been completed. After all, I was actively participating in this coach's mastermind as a life coach, with a mission to help women discover their true identity – Yet somewhere along the way, amidst my efforts to assist others, I had undergone my identity crisis.

Standing before the mirror, I confronted the person staring back at me, echoing the same question I had posed to countless others: "Who are you?" The deeper I delved into introspection, the more unfamiliar the reflection became. Once confident and accomplished, I now faced a stranger within myself. Where once stood a poised leader and overachiever, now stood someone small and broken. She didn't have a clue as to who she was or why she was there. Who was this person, and what had she done with me? As difficult as it was to stare into this stranger's eyes, I stood, determined to get the answers I sought. I closed my eyes, took a breath, and allowed myself to go deeper.

I found myself confronted with the numerous setbacks that life had dealt me over the years. Each recollection brought with it a weight of its own, from the diagnosis of high blood pressure at the tender age of 22 to the loss of my dream job, which led to the loss of my home, my car, and even my sense of dignity as I found myself sleeping in my car with nowhere else to turn. By the time I reached thirty, diabetes had become an unwelcome companion, one I was stuck with for the rest of my days. And just two years later, on what should have been an amazing honeymoon, I was blindsided by the loss of my sight. It soon became apparent that these countless losses had woven a narrative in my mind— I had adopted the identity of a loser. It wasn't until I experienced an unimaginable loss that plunged me to the lowest point of my life that I realized the depth of my despair.

"OH GOD, NOT AGAIN!" was the first thought that pierced my mind. As we sat there, my husband and I, hanging onto the doctor's every word, a sense of dread washed over us. His words, each one heavier than the last, unfolded like a tragic script, reshaping the trajectory of our lives forever. As he flipped through image after image, my heart grew weaker and weaker as I could no longer feel it beating. All I could feel was it breaking into a million pieces; there was nothing I could do to stop it. Each sentence seemed worse than the one before. The world around me blurred into darkness with everyone's voices fading to a distant echo. There were no words that I could conjure up, only tears cascading down my cheeks, each one a silent scream of disbelief. "This can't be happening," my soul cried out. "Not after all we've endured. It's too much, too cruel; this can't be real." As I felt my husband grab my hand, I knew it was real, and I wasn't dreaming; this nightmare was our reality. All I could do was sit there, numb, lost, broken to my core. With the bit of strength I had left, I grabbed my chest and whispered, "Breathe, Barbara, breathe."

It all started four months earlier when I felt something strange. In my mind, there was no doubt: this had to be the work of the devil or some spiritual attack. My certainty stemmed from recent events—I had just delivered a powerful sermon, leading many to accept Jesus Christ as their personal Savior. Besides, why else would I feel so dreadful? I immediately contacted my best friend, urging her to pray for me. But as I poured out my concerns to her, detailing my exhaustion, persistent nausea, and painfully swollen breasts, she responded with a chuckle. "Girl, you're not under attack," she said. "You're pregnant!" I balked at the idea, insisting it was impossible. After all, medical professionals had informed me that conception without assistance was out of the question. Yet, her words lingered in my mind, sowing a seed of doubt. Could it be true? Acting on impulse, I rushed to the store, purchased two pregnancy tests, and anxiously awaited the results. Almost immediately, they confirmed what we had never dared to imagine: we were expecting a child. It was a miracle—an unexpected gift from God, far beyond anything we had ever prayed for or anticipated. Despite enduring countless losses, this was undeniably a win.

During the 20-week anatomical scan, on what should have been one of the happiest days of our lives, my husband and I received the most devastating news expecting parents could imagine. Doctors discovered a severe issue with our son's heart. He was diagnosed with Pulmonary Atresia, a congenital disability where the valve controlling blood flow from the heart to the lungs fails to develop.

Facing this heartbreaking diagnosis, we were presented with three options. Option 1: We could continue with the pregnancy as usual, knowing that our son would have only hours to live after birth due to the inability to receive oxygen properly. Option 2: We could opt for potentially life-extending heart surgery after birth, but this would entail multiple procedures and a diminished quality of life. Option 3: We could choose to terminate the pregnancy, given the likely challenges our son would face if carried to term.

None of these options felt acceptable—they all seemed to lead to further heartache and loss. In desperation, I turned to prayer. I pleaded with God to heal my son, but also for the strength to accept whatever path lay ahead for us.

As I journeyed through my pregnancy with my son, I felt God's presence and heard His voice speak to me often. He revealed His promises concerning my children, assuring me of His plans. He showed me that while He would take my son and heal him in heaven, He would also fulfill His promise by sending me a daughter here on earth. I was devastated at the thought of losing my son, yet I found solace and peace in knowing that God's wisdom far surpassed my own. On April 13, 2012, Mac Henry Gentry III, affectionately known as "Judah." Was born. Despite the challenges, he graced our lives for seven days, departing on April 20, 2012, cradled in my arms.

Reliving the most painful day of my life, I found myself transported back to the very moment of Judah's passing. Seated in the same posture, I could feel the weight of his lifeless body in my arms, his tiny hand clasped tightly in mine as I watched him draw his final breaths. The urge to escape this agonizing memory overwhelmed me, yet an unyielding force compelled me to confront it head-on. I remember feeling so conflicted; in one instance, I felt so relieved that he was no longer suffering, and then the next, I felt so angry that I wouldn't get a chance to be his mommy. I wrestled with the divine plan that had swiftly turned a miracle into a tragedy. Through tear-filled eyes, I could only whisper, "Why must this be one more thing I survive?" Something happened. Those familiar words echoed in my mind, but this time, they hit differently. "I survived! I survived!" Despite enduring the most profound loss imaginable, I had not been defeated.

On the contrary, I survived! With this newfound clarity, I began to believe in my ability to rewrite the narrative of my life, to shed the burdensome labels that had weighed me down for so long. In that transformative moment, I resolved to infuse my pain with purpose. I recognized that my destiny awaited, and it was time to embrace my true identity.

I jumped up from that position, grabbed my journal, and pleaded with God to guide me through this process. Show me how to bounce back after hitting rock bottom and losing it all. In that moment, I began my journey of recovery. With a renewed mindset, I was determined to shed my self-limiting beliefs and embrace my royal identity. I realized that playing small was never my destiny; I was meant to stand tall and shine brightly.

And the same holds true for you. Regardless of how far you've fallen or the losses you've endured, you can bounce back just as I did. As stated in Deuteronomy 28:13a, "And the Lord shall make thee the head, and not the tail; and thou shalt be above only, and thou shalt not be beneath." Essentially, we are destined to lead, not reside at the bottom. It is our time to bounce back from the bottom to the boss!

Keys To Bouncing Back: Prioritize What's Important

By following these strategies, you can also overcome your current situation and start living the life you aspire to. An essential step in this journey is a simple exercise. First grab a sheet of paper and number it one through five. Now, list your top five priorities in order of importance. Next, close your eyes and take a moment to reflect on how you spent the last 24 hours of your time. Afterward, compare your list with your activities. Did your time investments align with your priorities? Did you devote more time to things not on your list? Most importantly, did you include yourself among your priorities? Did you include yourself on the list?

Your top five priorities should receive most of your time and attention. Anything not on the list should only occupy the remaining time after addressing your priorities. Interestingly, in my experience working with various groups of women, I've noticed a common trend: many forget to include themselves on the list. Even when they do, the time they invest in themselves often falls short of the importance they place on themselves. This tendency is pervasive among women, as we are naturally inclined to nurture and give to others. However, it's crucial to remember to replenish ourselves amidst our caregiving roles. We must recognize that we can only show up as our best selves for others once we ensure that we show up for ourselves. Airlines illustrate this principle by instructing us to secure our own oxygen masks before assisting others—an essential reminder often forgotten in moments of crisis. Instead, we slap that 'S' on our chest, jump into our Superwoman role, and are off to save the day.

I vividly recall when one of my coaching sisters enlightened me about this pattern when I felt burnt out, overwhelmed, and depleted. She told me, "Sis, you can't pour from an empty cup. You must remember the cup is for you, and the saucer which contains the overflow is for others". These words resonated deeply and provided much-needed clarity. Regrettably, we frequently overlook these principles when faced with a loved one's distress, feeling compelled to prioritize their needs over ours. Like many women, I was pouring from an empty cup, depletin" myself in the process. I was giving what I didn't have to give because I was forgetting to put myself on the list. By neglecting to prioritize ourselves, we diminish our worth and hinder our ability to become the best versions of ourselves. Therefore, the 'Irst crucial step in bouncing back from adversity is to prioritize Self-care and ensure we're on our own list of priorities.

The next step represents the most pivotal actions essential for bouncing back from the bottom to the boss. In this step, you must identify and commit to the concept of the D.R.E.A.M.

Destiny

Recognized

Eagerly

Anticipating

Manifestation

Before you embark on your journey of recovery, it is vital that you have unwavering faith as to where you are headed. As the acronym suggests, when you embrace D.R.E.A.M., you recognize that a God-ordained destiny awaits you, and you eagerly anticipate its manifestation.

Equally crucial is understanding the "WHY" behind your commitment. Your "WHY" serves as the driving force propelling you toward your destiny, even amidst life's adversities that may challenge your beliefs. This becomes especially important when what you are experiencing in real life looks the opposite of the destiny revealed to you in your D.R.E.A.M. You have a real adversary who will try everything to get you to abandon your journey. I realized this is what was happening to me during my season of persistent loss. Instead of steadfastly adhering to the vision and promises God had given me, I fell victim to the narrative the enemy presented, falsely portraying it as my destiny.

Overcoming Hurdles

I discovered that there are five hurdles you must overcome to pursue your destiny fully. These subtle obstacles can easily masquerade as integral parts of your dream. Interestingly, when arranged them, their initial letters spell out the word "dream." However, rather than propelling you toward your destiny, they're poised to derail your vision before it fully materializes prematurely. These hurdles include:

Disguised Distractions—These distractions manifest as people, places, things, and circumstances are intentionally sent to divert you from your path. They could emerge through losing a loved one, failed relationships, job setbacks, shattered commitments, or any challenges designed to shift your focus away from your goals and trap you in their accompanying emotions. Be vigilant against these distractions!

Rescued Reality—This obstacle poses the most formidable challenge as it appears when you're most vulnerable. Consider this scenario: a new job opportunity arises, promising extra income to help alleviate your overdue bills. However, it demands more time, diverting your focus from your dreams to fuel someone else's aspirations. Alternatively, it might present itself as a quick fix to a predicament, tempting you to stray from the path already revealed to you by God. The rescued reality often masquerades as a hero, but truthfully, it robs you of experiences, opportunities, and connections vital to your destiny.

Error in Estimating Tim—This obstacle, arguably, is the most treacherous. It deceives you into believing you have more time than reality permits. It manifests through procrastination and hesitation, leading individuals to delay tasks they could accomplish today. Sadly, many dreams have perished at this point because their owner made an error in estimating how much time they had left to fulfill their destiny.

Absence of Accountability—This obstacle is difficult for most people because, instinctively, most individuals shy away from being answerable to others. In addition, the enemy's deception may convince you that silence is the key. You may believe you should conceal your dreams for one of two reasons: fear that someone else will steal them or the lack of belief that they will come true. Yet, it would help if you shared your dream with someone you trust. This could be a friend, family member, mentor, or coach who can recognize and believe in your destiny just as much as you do. In addition, you need someone who can hold you to your WHY when your faith begins to waver. Their support and guidance could mean the difference between abandoning the mission and manifesting your promise.

The Biggest Enemy—Lastly, represented by the letter "M," I symbolize the final obstacle. I have found that my biggest enemy is 'in-a-me'! Stifling thoughts, limiting beliefs, insecurities, and excuses hinder our progress on the path to recovery. Recognizing and overcoming these internal barriers is essential for success.

The Power of Belief

The empowering truth is that you hold the key to unlocking your destiny. The bridge between recognizing your purpose and seeing it come to fruition lies in two simple words: Eagerly Anticipating. This concept, rooted in the power of anticipation, is pivotal in your journey toward manifestation. Anticipation, as defined by vocabulary.com, is the eager feeling you experience while awaiting something you know will happen. When I first encountered this definition, excitement coursed through me. Suddenly, God flooded my thoughts with every dream, desire, and promise bestowed upon me. What was once seemingly out of reach now fell within grasp, filling me with an overwhelming sense of possibility.

Yet, amidst this excitement, doubt, and fear crept in, casting shadows on my dreams. It was a moment of profound realization: anticipation is a potent force that adapts to our beliefs and expectations. Unlike fleeting emotions such as happiness or worry, anticipation's emotional tone hinges entirely on our perspective and what we anticipate. Positive expectations breed pleasure and joy, while negative ones spawn stress and doubt. Thus, the pivotal question arises: what do you honestly believe?

In times of adversity, it is not enough to rely on fleeting emotions; we must anchor ourselves in unwavering faith. The Word of God, particularly Romans 8:28, offers profound insight: "And we know that all things work together for the good of those who love God, who are called according to his purpose." This scripture guides our journey, fortifying our hearts and minds against the trials that test our faith. By activating this scripture as the cornerstone of our anticipation, we can stand firm in the face of adversity, kn"wing that all things are working together for our good. With this foundation, we can silence the negative voices of doubt and fear, confidently awaiting the manifestation of our destiny. Our divine purpose will come to fruition as the chosen ones.

Boss Thoughts

As I look back on the different chapters of my life's journey, I recognize the role of anticipation and the guiding light found in Romans 8:28. I must admit there were many instances where I failed to see how these challenges worked for my benefit. In truth, I often felt that each trial was stealing away my destiny rather than contributing to it. I vividly remember being diagnosed with high blood pressure at the young age of 22, feeling like I was too young to be burdened with such a condition. Similarly, when I was diagnosed with diabetes at 30 and later with sleep apnea, I couldn't help but question why these challenges had to be a part of my life.

However, armed with the wisdom of Romans 8:28, my perspective began to shift. I remained committed to God's dreams and promises, eagerly anticipating that each challenge would somehow work in my favor. And indeed, they did.

Looking back with hindsight, I realized that without my son's medical condition, which surprisingly helped regulate my existing health issues, my precious daughter, Brielle Latressa Tamar Gentry, would not be with us today. Similarly, when I contracted COVID-19 in 2021 and was instructed to quarantine at home, I found myself in a difficult situation. Despite being quite ill, I didn't meet the criteria for hospitalization. In those uncertain times, I turned to prayer and sought divine guidance.

God assured me that I still had a purpose and destiny to fulfill, and it was up to me to determine my posture and mindset while facing the uncertainty of my health. I chose to anticipate healing and the fulfillment of my destiny eagerly. In a remarkable turn of events, God reminded me of the medical equipment I had accumulated over the years, which I could use to monitor my vitals at home.

It was a surreal moment when I realized I had access to tools that hospitals lacked. Once again, Romans 8:28 manifested itself in my life. Every diagnosis, every medical device, and every trial I had endured since the age of 22 were now converging to work together for my good. What

I once saw as obstacles threatening my life became the means through which my life was preserved.

Upon reflection, I realized every setback was a steppingstone toward greater heights. Despite facing challenges that tested my resolve and forced me to confront my doubts and fears head-on, I remained steadfast, refusing to abandon my dreams despite the obstacles in my path.

Success is far from a linear journey filled with twists, turns, ups, and downs. The true differentiator between those who succeed and those who do not lies in their circumstances but in their mindset—their ability to perceive opportunity in adversity and to transform setbacks into setups for success.

I believed I had cracked the code on bouncing back from rock bottom to boss status many years ago when I transitioned from homelessness to owning a beautiful home or moved from unemployment to becoming the C.F.O. of a prominent nonprofit. However, I understood that being a boss is not defined by titles or possessions; it is rooted in mindset and belief. As the saying goes, "As a person thinks, so they become." The journey from the bottom to the boss was not solely about overcoming adversity but cultivating a mindset of resilience, determination, and unwavering belief.

Embracing this new mindset led to a profound transformation in my definition of success. Success was no longer solely measured by external achievements or material possessions; it became intricately linked to the person I became throughout my journey. It became about the depth of my character, the strength of my spirit, and the resilience of my heart.

I realized that success is not just an outcome but a continuous journey of growth, self-discovery, and inner fulfillment. It is about overcoming obstacles, embracing challenges, and remaining true to my values and convictions, even in the face of adversity. This shift in perspective redirected my focus from fleeting achievements to enduring qualities, from momentary victories to lasting impact.

As you continue your journey from the bottom to the boss, remember to carry the lessons learned along the way—the importance of prioritizing yourself, the power of mindset and belief in shaping your destiny, and the resilience needed to overcome life's challenges. Ultimately, what matters most is not where you start or end up but the journey you undertake and the person you become along the way.

Let's
Go
DEEPER!

Facing Your Past

What are some instances where confronting past hurts or losses has led to personal growth or transformation?

_____

_____

_____

_____

_____

_____

_____

_____

_____

_____

When you look in the mirror, who do you see? Has your perception of yourself changed over time?

_____

_____

_____

_____

_____

_____

_____

_____

_____

_____

Bouncing Back

In what ways can the concept of "putting yourself on the list" be applied to various aspects of life?

_____

_____

_____

_____

_____

_____

_____

_____

_____

_____

Reflect on the concept of the D.R.E.A.M. Do you have a clear understanding of your destiny, and are you eagerly anticipating its manifestation despite any current adversities?

_____

_____

_____

_____

_____

_____

_____

_____

_____

Overcoming Hurdles

Consider the importance of accountability in your journey towards fulfilling your destiny. Have you shared your dreams and aspirations with someone you trust for support and guidance?

_____

_____

_____

_____

_____

_____

_____

_____

_____

Reflecting on the "Me, myself, and I" obstacle, can you recognize any self-limiting beliefs or negative thought patterns that have held you back from reaching your full potential?

_____

_____

_____

_____

_____

_____

_____

_____

_____

The Power of Belief

Reflect on the concept of the journey from the bottom to the boss. What lessons have you learned along the way about the importance of prioritizing yourself, nurturing a positive mindset, and cultivating resilience?

_____

_____

_____

_____

_____

_____

_____

_____

_____

_____

_____

_____

_____

_____

_____

_____

_____

_____

_____

_____

Navigating Your Life's Compass

Rhonda H. Thompson, PhD

Navigating your life's compass involves aligning your actions with your values and goals. It requires you to regularly assess your direction, adjust your course if needed, and stay true to your principles. This intentional navigation leads to a more purposeful and fulfilling life. I have found this to be true during each phase of my life.

Excellence cannot be achieved through osmosis. Proximity to high achievers provides inspiration, but you must put in the work to push through challenges and elevate your personal standards. As a child, I remember being interested in knowing more and doing more. When I realized that I had the talent for drawing and sketching, I began to teach myself how to perfect that talent. The internet did not exist, we did not have a computer, and we were not aware of anyone who taught drawing classes. It was the 80's, and if you grew up in a small town like me, lessons for hobbies were not always available or sought after. You were expected to "figure it out." I shifted my compass towards a talent. While in junior high school, I made the high school cheer squad. This was certainly an exciting accomplishment for me since I was thought to be quiet or shy. What I learned later about myself is that I always attracted attention even when I did not want it, so I began to say less and shrink my presence. I did not want to be the center of attention. Well, as a cheerleader and later captain of the squad, that is exactly what happened; I became the center of attention every week. More importantly, it enhanced my understanding of my ability to be a leader and appreciate the gift of influence. I realized that if you are doing positive things and saying inspirational words, it is okay for people to be interested in what you are doing. Exposure to new things can help you expand your thoughts and motivate you to develop multiple skills. You will also recognize some of your inherent skills just waiting to grow.

Internal Drive

I grew up in a two-parent household with my siblings. I have a great appreciation for family and the joy that comes from experiencing supportive family members. We were not a warm and cozy family with "I love you" being stated daily, but I learned at an early age that personal standards that align with your morals and values help you build a sturdy sense of self. Knowing that you have family members who care about your well-being, your personal growth, and how you present yourself in the world is something that cannot be bought. Perfect relationships do not exist. Everyone must give time and energy to make meaningful connections.

My internal drive to succeed and achieve excellence was fueled by the potential for me to do things that I had not heard about or seen. If I joined an organization, participated in a sketch contest, made the run-through signs for the football team, or was a Young Woman of the Year contestant, I set goals of excellence for myself. My academic performance was great, and I did not see any reason to be mediocre when I could strive for excellence. Now, this did not mean that I did not experience doubt, nervousness, or others voicing skepticism. Somehow, the unknown did not keep me from trying to quiet the "what if you fail" voice that arose from time to time. That voice can creep up at any age. I decided to turn my compass needle toward excellence.

As I matriculated through high school, I continued to learn how I could position myself to gain knowledge. Although, I did not have anyone in my family who completed a college degree, I knew that it was the right path for me. I attended and graduated from the historic Tuskegee University with a Bachelor of Science degree. While I was a student, I served as a leader and a campus queen in different capacities. I experienced some setbacks, but I was determined to push through. I was commissioned as a military intelligence officer in the United States Army. The leadership skills and discipline that I gained as a military officer were invaluable. Those skills are still prevalent today.

Marriage and Motherhood

My compass needle moved again. My journey in life led me to marry my husband, who was also an officer in the United States Army. Eventually, the demands of the dual military life forced me to make some decisions about how I wanted to raise my children. I remembered my personal standards and value for family life and decided that I would no longer serve in the armed forces. For the next 15 years, I devoted my primary time and effort to my family and three children.

Well, you know me, during that time I needed to continue to find a way to keep growing and moving. As a military spouse, the sacrifice and time can sometimes cause you to rethink your choices. I wondered how I was going to inspire others and set an example of excellence for my children. Through prayer and much thought, I set out on a path to master my power and keep moving forward. I later earned a Master of Science degree in counseling psychology and Doctor of Philosophy degree in general psychology. I served in organizations that provided community service; I created workshops for youth and young adults while maintaining a schedule that allowed me to support my family at a high level.

Change and Motivation

After I completed my doctoral degree, I was in search of a way to convey my mastery mindset teachings to others. I began to incorporate my skills and knowledge from my military experience with the research and knowledge that I gained as a mental health professional. I also began to instruct college courses as an adjunct professor. A basic part of my purpose in life is to help others; one of those ways is sharing knowledge about self-mastery. The idea of self-mastery described my mastery mindset to perfection. Self-Mastery helps you to be a better version of you so that you can discover whom you can be.

I did the work and firmly believe that self-mastery is within everyone's reach. It encompasses the ability to take full control of one's thoughts, behavior, and overall presentation. To facilitate this process, I have created a comprehensive self-mastery toolkit designed to address the gaps that may have emerged due to life transitions and the challenges associated with multiple roles. I teach coping tactics, mindfulness techniques, conflict resolution skills, unconventional leadership approaches, personal presentation skills, and relationship-building techniques. You may be holding on to habits that do not provide positive outcomes. You can master the power within you. I know that you have this power because the Creator made you EXCELLENT and its time to acknowledge it and be about the business of YOU.

Mastering Your Compass

Determine where your compass is leading you. Are you ensuring that it aligns with your values and goals? I am going to share 3 of my steps to begin your self-mastery journey:

> **Step 1. Become a more congruent person.** This means that the person *who you desire to be* and the person *whom you actually have* good overlap. The difference between the two

should not be extensive. People often wear different masks in different settings; they code switch to suit diverse groups like friends, co-workers, family members. Sometimes they turn on the professional switch at 9am, turn it off at 5pm, and they are a completely different person for the rest of the day.

If that sounds like you, I am going to offer an alternative. Make sure that you include the authentic you in your daily interactions. You reduce the stress of having to perform as a character in a setting. After all, who wants to play a character role during everyday interactions? Develop an authentic presentation that you can be comfortable sharing with people in any setting.

Step 2. Accept the fact that change is inevitable. Have the personal resilience to lean in on change. You may be going through a difficult life transition right now. You may be building your career, starting your family, or adapting to college life. Mastering change requires adaptability. Stay open to new possibilities. Developing resilience and learning from experiences can help you navigate and thrive amidst change. Stay flexible while adapting to a positive mindset. Stay focused on what you can control and ask for support from others when you need it. I experienced personal growth when I began viewing change as another opportunity for adaptability.

Change is one of the primary types of stress experienced by most people. The way in which you deal with change speaks to your resilience and tolerance for stress.

Step 3. Develop a coping plan for stress. Understand what causes stress in your life. The primary causes of stress include:

- **Frustration**- blocked goals
- **Conflict**- incompatible (desirable and undesirable) motivations
- **Change**- needing to adapt to social adjustments or life changes
- **Pressure**- to perform or conform.

These causes of stress, ultimately, manifest as types of stress:

- **Physical stress**- over or under exercising; muscle tension, headaches, fatigue
- **Mental stress**- verbal or mental abuse; taking on too many responsibilities; feeling overly anxious
- **Nutritional stress**- eating too much, too little, or the wrong proportions
- **Thermal stress**- adjusting to seasonal changes and temperature changes
- **Chemical stress**- lack of vitamin D usually obtained from sunlight; exposure to internal and external toxins (i.e., drug use, alcohol, environmental pollutions, smoking)

Mastering stress involves adopting coping mechanisms like deep breathing, time management, and setting realistic goals. Be mindful of how negative self-talk and destructive criticism can hinder your ability to master stress. Regular exercise, adequate sleep, and maintaining a positive mindset contribute to stress resilience. Additionally, you can 1) practice mindfulness, 2) seek social support, 3) set boundaries with others, and 4) take breaks when needed.

Surviving the Jungle of Corporate America

Deidre Miller

"Though I walk through the valley of the shadow of death, I shall fear no evil, for thou are with me." This was my morning mantra as I reported to my job in Corporate America; the job that took me over the edge. It was my wake-up call that almost killed me. I mean literally. I recall that day like it was on a movie reel running through my head. I remember dragging myself out of bed, slightly tired and a bit sluggish. I thought it was just me not getting enough rest the night before. I turned on the shower to the hottest setting I could withstand; hot water has always given me energy; however, that day felt just a little different. It was as if my body was rejecting the energy. I continued to get dressed, not knowing what the day might bring. After getting dressed and heading out the door, I logged into an 8:30 am meeting as I typically would in my car while driving to the "Valley of the Shadow of Death." As I logged into the conference call, I could feel my heart starting to beat faster than normal. I began talking to myself, "Just breathe. Take deep breaths." As I continued to drive. I had a short distance to go, so I placed my phone on mute and continued taking deep breaths while listening to the office's chaos and confusion. I pulled up to the parking lot of my job, and I sat there for a moment. Trying to get my body mentally and physically ready to walk into the "Valley of Shadow of Death." (You probably wonder why I keep calling it the "Valley of the Shadow of Death." Just hold on; I will get to how my last Corporate America job earned this title.) I got out of my car with my laptop and bags in hand that I would use to hold my purse and all the medications I would need to get through my regular 10-hour day of constant confusion and the chaos amongst management on how to resolve all the technical issues we were experiencing because they did not heed the warnings my team and I shared with them months back during phase one of a new global software implementation. The tension was so thick you could cut it with a knife, and emotions were extremely high. It was argument after argument. Every day, I would walk through those dreaded doors, and it was like stepping lightly through a war zone with mines waiting to go off. In conversations, you had to tread lightly and choose your words carefully as you did not want to ignite an already short-fused upper management. I was going from meeting to meeting with people wanting to understand why they did not receive adequate training, wondering how they would do their jobs, and whether the system would effectively do what we paid millions of dollars to do. Two hours passed, and roughly around 10:30 am, I started feeling light-headed and dizzy. It was the onset of an anxiety attack that had been plaguing my life for the last few months; hence, why I had to carry around a medicine cabinet in my purse. I had to stop dead in the middle of a meeting with another team member and find the next dosage of medicine I needed to take to quiet the symptoms so I could continue trying to function in a chaotic and toxic environment for anyone who is just slightly sane. The medicine took effect, but it only lasted for another hour and a half. The first anxiety attack was just the preliminary warm-up. I had another meeting to go to at 11 am, and during this meeting, I started feeling my previous symptoms again, but this time with a vengeance. My heart started racing like a car in the Indie 500. The beats of my heart seemed so loud my ears were pulsating. I was looking up at the video conference screen, and all my mind could comprehend was that mouths were moving, but I could not mentally connect the sound with the mouth movement. Luckily, the meeting ended quickly! I stood up very slowly because I was light-headed, and new symptoms showed up. My left arm started tingling, followed by sharp, needle-piercing pain going down my arm. On the outside, I tried to appear calm, but on the inside, all kinds of medical diagnoses were running through my head. Am I having a stroke or a heart attack? What is happening? I slowly walked, holding and squeezing my arm, into the kitchen to get a drink of water, knowing that would not soothe anything now. My arm began to go numb, and my leg started to tingle, so I leaned up against the kitchen wall for a moment. I saw the team member I was in a meeting with earlier. She asked, "Are you ok?" I said, "My left arm and leg are going numb." She replied, "You need to go home!" I staggered back to my desk, and by then, I felt excruciating pain going up and down my arm to the point that I could not raise it. I sat down, contemplating whether to drive to the emergency room or call 911. Well, my body decided for me. My hand began to turn blue. I knew then it was time to call 911. I was still trying to remain calm in my outer appearance, but I was scared to death that I was repeating what had happened to me ten years ago. I thought I was having yet another stroke almost ten years to the date. My manager looked at me and asked, "Do you want me to take you to the emergency room?" I said, "No, you better call 911!" An ambulance came right away, but by the time they arrived, my entire left side had gone numb, including the left side of my face and mouth. Consequently, I had a hotel stay in a great hospital for two days. I thank God every day that I did not have another stroke, but the symptoms were stroke-like and diagnosed as a severe panic attack with acute left-sided weakness.

I never knew anything about battling anxiety or panic attacks until I worked at my last Corporate America job. A few months back, a young lady died of a heart attack, and I did not want to be another victim who succumbed to an overwhelmingly unhealthy, robotic operating mentality and work ethic that had penetrated the outer and inner layers of my humanity without thought of self. I was just trying to be an outstanding employee and financially sustain my household and family. Unfortunately, the harsh reality of it all is if something had happened to me, I would have just been replaced with another number and butt in a seat and then back to business as usual. That is how my last job earned the name "The Valley of Shadow of Death!" this environment had already claimed one hard-working woman, and I did not want to be the next victim.

After a short stint in the hospital, I knew it was time to do something different. I could not continue to function in an environment that was not conducive to my physical or mental health. I do not recommend that you make the same exit as I did. I was forced to leave due to a medical condition that was caused by constantly working in a high stress, hostile working environment with so many close calls to death. At some point, it should not take medical scare after medical scare to know when it is time to call it quits. I decided it was time to come up with some sort of plan. I thought to myself what a way to make an exit from the jungles of Corporate America. After being in Corporate America for twenty-eight years, I had made the decision to leave and do something that made me happy for once and figure out a way to create my own economy which led me to create these 3 strategies on how to make a successful that resembles a farmer's way of preparing for a new crop.

STRATEGY #1:

Plowing the Soil—Plowing the soil is an agricultural term that means preparing the ground by removing dead weeds, old plants, or crops and breaking up the soil to make room for new seeds to grow. When I decided to leave Corporate America, I knew that I had to be able to prepare physically, mentally, and emotionally to do something different and attempt to cultivate my inner soil for a new phase in my life, which was going to take some time. I recommend taking at least a week of vacation or longer to clear your mind so you can make a sound decision and not an emotional one unless there is a health crisis, as was in my case. We often do not realize how we must desperately decompress all the physical and mental stressors that happen throughout a typical workday or week; especially, if you are in management and have people reporting to you. Usually, you carry both your team and your issues, too, because your team can reflect your leadership or management attributes.

I realized I needed an outlet to dispel all that was going on with me physically, mentally, and psychologically because I kept replaying the events in my head repeatedly, which led me to this moment. I kept asking myself if I really wanted to leave this job and the financial stability, bonuses, benefits, and perks that came with it. Even after this last medical scare, I still struggled with leaving it all behind and identifying what was important to me. My health or my money? My sanity or my money? Those were conversations I was having with myself as I was planning my exit strategy. There were plenty of tossing and turning, sleepless nights. I wondered how I would get these thoughts out of my head that caused me even more stress and anxiety trying to figure it out. I decided to purchase a journal or use a computer to document any emotional or non-emotional thoughts, feelings, or ideas that came to me while I was on medical leave.

I had to find a place of solitude to process all the events that had occurred, so I chose a place that was quiet and relaxing. This helped me to focus inward on clearing my mind, relaxing my body, and refreshing my inner spirit, which laid dormant for a while due to all the stress and mental and physical exhaustion. Refreshing my inner spirit was me trying to reconnect with God and the inner workings of my intuition or whoever you consider your higher power. I started a meditation routine where I would pull up a self-guided meditation video on YouTube or sit quietly for at least 15 to 20 minutes or longer in the morning and at night. I recommend turning off or muting all devices so there are no distractions during your meditation. If you have never meditated before, start with a minimum of 10 minutes, and add more time as needed. When I first started, I noticed my mind was everywhere. Meditation is supposed to quiet the mind. My mind told me I needed coffee, needed to eat breakfast, or to check my phone. You get the picture. It took me a few meditation sessions of sitting with myself until I recognized that I had to sit there long enough until the noise shut down in my mind. Trying to quiet the noise in my head was like telling Alexa to turn down loud music playing in my house. I experienced many benefits when I meditated. I noticed after beginning my meditation routine that it helped reduce my anxiety and stress levels and improve my focus, and I was not as irritable. Also, it helped me stay calm and manage my emotions better. I was reunited with my inner spirit, which helped me gain spiritual and mental clarity, declutter negative energy, and rid myself of the corporate residue causing my body to break down from the inside out like a car that needed a new motor. I am not religious, but I am very spiritual, and your mind, body, and spirit must be aligned. I firmly believe in the quote I share with my clients: *"Your power, strength, confidence, and healing start in the mind!"*.

Once I realized that I had to plow the soil for new seeds to grow, my spirit's healing and rejuvenation began. It meant I had to dispel all the old feelings and emotions of self-doubt of not being good enough, worthy enough, smart enough, and being overworked and underpaid. I had to rid myself of the old Corporate America residue that managed to penetrate my spirit's outer barriers after being passed up or overlooked for promotions, fighting for leadership or management positions, and my seat at the table. I had to cast aside the damage of being constantly judged by my surface appearance, including the paper that lists my education and other credentials, and not being recognized for the exceptional asset and undeniable value I bring to any company that decided to hire me.

Strategy#2:

Getting Ready for a New Harvest—It was time to prepare for a new harvest. Farmers must devise a plan on how they will harvest their crops once the seeds are planted. In my efforts to create a new harvest for myself, I quickly discovered I did not have a clue as to what the next steps were to exit Corporate America. For my sanity, this exit strategy needed to be a well-thought-out, purposeful plan. I had to really be honest with myself. What exactly was I going to do once I left corporate America? All these years being codependent on receiving a paycheck every other week. Here are just a few of the questions I begin asking myself. Am I prepared for the mental impact of this career change? What do I enjoy doing, can I monetize it? If so, can I be fulfilled doing it? Will this change affect my identity and sense of self-worth? How will I manage the financial transition of leaving a steady corporate job? What does my ideal work life look like, and how can I achieve it? It really made me rethink if I was truly mentally prepared for this new journey I was about to embark upon. When you have been working for someone else for most of your life or at least half your life, like me, it will be quite the transition. When I purchased my journal, I did not do it just to write down all mental noise going on in my head and the financial aspects of the transition, but also to write down everything I enjoyed doing. It was time to look inward because I knew this was going to help me lay the foundation, mentally and physically, to begin designing a new phase in my life; as well as help me envision my ideal work scenario, whether it involves entrepreneurship, freelance work, part-time employment, or a completely different field. While putting things into perspective and journaling, I realized that all of my transferable skills and valuable experiences I had gained could be applied to future endeavors. In addition, with the new perspective gained, I discovered my desired lifestyle, personal interests, and work-life balance aspirations.

I must admit it was scary in the beginning knowing that I was going to walk away from a successful 28-year professional career. However, what tipped the scale for me was that I was tired of giving my power away, being undervalued, working myself close to death, literally, and helping someone fulfill or accomplish their dreams instead of focusing on my own. As I began the process of diminishing the corporate residue that plagued and occupied my physical and mental space, I realized that a 28-year career built my strength, courage, perseverance, determination, and resilience muscle which prepared me for the next phase in my life. I had to come to terms with several aspects of this new journey. At first, I questioned whether this was a good move or not. For a minute, well, honestly, a few days, I thought I was losing my mind. The fear of the unknown crept in and tried to make me reconsider my decision to leave. I remember thinking, "Are you crazy?" Are you sure you want to do this? Are you willing to lose everything? Are you really going to take that risk? How are you going to take care of yourself and your family? What are you going to do for money? All the fear-driven negative self-talk is designed to protect you from danger, remind you of things you have never done before, or just a caution mechanism that you can either allow to deter you from making a decision or put fear in your pocket and let it tag along, knowing that it is there, but keep moving forward. I have always told my inner circle and clients that on the other side of fear, there could be blessings you never encounter if you do not take a leap of faith. Fear is only a way to avoid the discomfort of the unknown and your growth if you let it. However, fear can be reframed and replaced with the insight of awareness. I had to break through the negative thoughts running through my mind like an old song on repeat. I had to flip the negative self-talk song playing loudly in my head into an upbeat, high-energy melody such as "Living My Life Like It's Golden!" by Jill Scott, a Neo-Soul singer and actress.

There were still a few questions roaming around in my head. What would I do with all the time I would have, not working the typical 9-5 job? How would I use all that knowledge I gained over the years from working in multiple industries? How was I going to pay my bills consistently?

During one of my meditation sessions, I just sat with myself, closed my eyes, and tuned out the usual noise. My mind began to take me to the most beautiful and serene place where it seemed as though I was surrounded by air-defying angels with eagle-like, white feathery wings in a very calm and peaceful space as if we were playing in the clouds where I sat in the very center of this indescribable place. This vast circle of light shined down on me as if I were on a stage. There I sat in a trance with my arms raised high as I was ready to receive whatever was about to happen, and it felt as though the light was summoning me. I heard plain as day, "Teach the people!" I begin to look around, still in a transcendental state, asking myself, "Did I really hear that?" I heard the voice again. This time, louder, "Teach the people!" So, I responded out loud, how do I do that? Everything went quiet as a mouse, and then I woke up abruptly! My meditation seemed so real that it almost scared me. Some people say that when you pray, you are asking GOD, or your higher power, questions, and when you meditate, you get the answers. I am not trying to place my spiritual beliefs on anyone, but I received confirmation or a revelation of the next phase of my life. That is when I received my "ah-ha moment!"

It all became very clear that I had already been teaching through all the leadership and management roles I held in my Corporate America

Career, and it was now time to take my power back. With almost thirty years of conditioning and teaching my staff, and sometimes, the managers above me, it was time to venture out into the world. This moment gave me the courage to move my life one step forward and beyond my comfort level. It gave me the idea that I could get a new canvas and design my future. Stand up and be the director of my life and no longer just a supporting actress. Believe in and bet on myself, fulfill my dreams, and stop funding other people's dreams. Decide to pivot and explore the unknown path to greatness with faith and bravery because that is what happens when you walk in your divine purpose.

Strategy #3:

> **Excavation**—This would not be an easy task even though I had rehearsed it plenty of times. I had gone over everything in my head a million times as if I were auditioning for a new role in a movie. It still felt uncomfortable, almost as if I was letting my staff down and feeling slightly sorry for leaving them with a mess to clean up that the company had created. However, I had to shift my mind to look at all the health challenges I endured as the result of a very reactive, flying-by-the-seat-of-their-pants type working environment that almost played a pivotal role in my demise and leaving my family and friends behind. I had to snap out of that crazy chatter in my head quickly.

Resigning from a job is a significant decision, so several important factors must be considered to ensure a seamless transition. My father always told me never to burn bridges you may have to go back across, so remember that how you handle your resignation can impact your professional reputation and/or future opportunities. As a mental note, wherever you work or whatever position you hold and you decide to resign, just do it with care, professionalism, and respectfulness whenever possible. I know sometimes that may not be the case with some jobs. I have been there too!

It was time for my journey to end in the Corporate America jungle. It would be my last walk through the "Valley of the shadow of death". It was a virtual walk due to my medical condition; nevertheless, I held my head high as I threw up the surrender flag, not literally, but that is what it felt like as I was preparing the email and attaching my resignation. It would be the longest two weeks of my life; however, I felt a sense of relief and weight being removed from my spiritual body along with a freedom to pursue my dreams and fulfill my life purpose now finally. What I have truly learned from this 28-year journey was that I am stronger than ever. Sometimes you must funeralize certain parts of your existence to step into your greatness. Things, people, or relationships including business relationships that no longer serve you must be left behind for your new season to arrive. I am so grateful for the experience as it prepared me for the Deidre 3.0 version. The speaker, author, transformational life coach and founder, CEO, 365 Elevate LLC, walking in my divine purpose.

Now, that I am walking in my divine purpose, I am creating a platform to assist woman around the world to get out of their own way, stop being paralyzed by fear, and unlock the mental prison in their minds that anchors them to unworthiness, doubt, and insecurities. Where the scars of every heartbreak, every failure, every moment of self-doubt are recognized as medals of their resilience. They are evidence of their ability to survive, to fight, and to emerge stronger. Each woman will begin to reclaim their power and step into their ideal life. Now, they can stop chasing their dreams and live them; and, see the world through a different lens called, "My most abundant life!". Where fulfillment is no longer in question, and they wake up with a beautiful smile on their face and in pure bliss as they embrace the journey to their future.

Go DEEPER:

This book was written to serve as an inspirational catalyst for women to not let the pressure and stressors of life weigh you down, or internalize it, and suffer in silence because it shows up as sickness in the body. It can impact your family and other relationships. To have the courage to pivot, take a step back to reassess your life no matter what age and to simply ask yourself a few questions to determine if you are living your best life or are you simply existing, going with the flow, living for other people, or vicariously living through other people? Do not be paralyzed by fear. Take fear and put it in your pocket as you recognize it is there and take the leap of faith as your blessings are on the other side waiting. Start being the director of your own movie and not the supporting actress.

Can you honestly say that you are happy in all aspects of your life, relationships, job, etc.? If you hesitate on any part of this question or if the answer is "no", then that is where you begin WWH Approach to unpack your answer. Why? What? How? Questions. Why am I not happy? What is standing in your way? How can I change it?

Take one aspect that is not working at this time. Contemplate these questions and journal your thinking here.

_____

_____

_____

_____

_____

_____

_____

_____

_____

_____

_____

_____

_____

_____

_____

_____

_____

_____

_____

Have you ever just sat down and wrote down what makes you happy, or things you enjoy doing, or things that get you excited to do? Could be cooking, writing, singing, drawing, painting, etc.?

_____

_____

_____

_____

_____

_____

_____

_____

Have I incorporated the things that make me happy into my life? If not, why not?

_____

_____

_____

_____

_____

_____

_____

_____

_____

These questions, if you answer them honestly, will get you started on the journey to the discovery of "You". You start to learn your life activators. Your life will begin to change when you walk in the true essence of You, your authentic self.

The Pink Epiphany

Lesli Odum

I am a Licensed Clinical Therapist, Certified Addictions Professional, Mental Health Trainer, and Speaker. However, I am not speaking to you from the authority of my titles. I am speaking to you as a sister, friend, wife, citizen of the kingdom, and mother in a posture of healing from my lived experience. My life experience has afforded me the insight, access, and connection neither my credentials nor education could offer.

I'm so glad you're here; the place where honesty, safety, and grace are requirements. I am hopeful that sharing my story will offer you some understanding of your, accelerate your healing process, and provide you with tools and strategies to live authentically; empowering you to access your inheritance in the kingdom.

Before we jump into my story, I want to be clear that I am not telling you that you can do what I have done—your story is different and uniquely designed for your specific purpose. I am *not* telling you to pull yourself up by your bootstraps. I am saying I used a variety of strategies that may be helpful to you. I encourage you to take what you need and apply it.

Overexposed, the one word I would use to describe my childhood. I saw, experienced, and heard things that are yet shaping my worldview. Emerging from them was a recurring theme. You name it, I cried about it because it happened to me, or someone I love. If you know anything about adverse childhood experience (ACES), you know that these could include divorce, separation, incarceration of a parent or caregiver, domestic violence, sexual abuse, poverty...you name it, I've seen it. So, I became unphased by these travesties. I moved through life, saying goodbye as I said hello. The socially engineered construct of the strong black women had swooped me up and embraced me tightly; and that worked for me, for a while. This strength took over my ability to ask questions, complain, be angry, have concern for myself, and address problems head-on. I was constantly comparing situations to everything I had seen, experienced, and heard. I had become numb—shielded myself from everything...phased by nothing. ***"This is nothing." Self-deception.*** I had not made a fuss about me.

I have been travailing for a while toward my better self. Here I am, continuing to heal through self-discovery, affirming my identity in Christ. I am what some call a learn-it-all. Thirsty for knowledge and exploring my passions, at the same time...healing to break intergenerational curses. I had just wrapped up my latest educational endeavor. My fiancé (now my husband) and I were looking to buy a house. We saw so many properties. We were on our second Real Estate Agent and now looking in an adjacent county from where we lived. I had grown so fatigued by the entire process. I was exhausted from looking and determined to find our 'home for now'. After a few months had passed, our Agent reached out with a few listings. We agreed to meet him at one of the house...the PINK house. As soon as we pulled into the driveway, I refused to go in. I had already decided from the outside that this was not our house. "I'll wait here." I said to my husband. I would save disagreements until we had privacy to talk it out, but this was just too much! That is how disgusted I was. *The house is pink...I hate pink*! Why would someone paint a house pink? For the life of me, I couldn't make myself understand. After some convincing, I went inside. I walked from room to room, trying to find other things I hated to my list. I was agonized; my list was short—there was not much that I did not like about the house. The inside had exactly what we needed. My husband said, "We can paint the house".

At this point in my life, I realized my disdain for pink. Here is what I came up with. In my mind, individuals who loved pink were too weak to recognize how strength was a benefit. All this time, I had associated pink with softness, delicateness, sensitivity, prissiness, deservingness, fragility, and tenderness. I did not feel I deserved all those attributes. I had to be strong. I was wrong. I began to laugh, cry, and pray at my epiphany to pink.

This narrative played a role in the background of my life for a long time. I had not realized it was there. That one question allowed me to begin seeking to understand myself and, in turn, identify my blind spots in my healing journey. After much digging, whew! My goal was to establish boundaries that teach me self-love and others how to treat me and promote respectful interactions. Here is where the inner therapist comes out. It set the tone for healthy communication, fostering understanding and cooperation in various aspects of my life. In essence, boundaries are not restrictions but the framework that enables me to navigate life with an intentional plan, ensuring that my actions align with my values and contribute to my overall well-being. I also desired to recognize and respect the boundaries of others to foster positive and harmonious relationships, the first relationship being myself. It includes having a particular standard of acceptable treatment.

The Epiphany of Pink

"We can paint the house". It was just that simple. Forced to explore the house, I found that there was absolutely nothing wrong with the house. Had I not taken the time to explore the house and everything that it offered, I would not have had the opportunity to get to know the house as a place of peace and solitude. The same way that I approached the house, I have learned, is the same way that faced myself; parked in the driveway of who I am, stuck in what was on the outside and not allowing myself or anyone else to discover what was inside.

I learned through the "pink house experience" that I was stuck in my own rigid thinking; blocking the very change that I needed. I was clinging onto what was safe. The pink paint on the outside of the house was very much like the external trappings that most of us grapple with— status, beauty, privacy; things that I often use as walls to keep people out.

The house made me face myself; loosening the grip that I had on my past—my old way of thinking, boundaries that no longer served me, and feelings that no longer fueled me.

To heal from trauma is to grieve. The pink house truly represented the soft blow of losing my old ways. It served as the segway that I needed to finally stand up the ACES and grieve who I thought I had to be. It carried me through the process of grief and led me to my ultimate healing.

Before the pink house epiphany, I truly lived in the shell of a house. The framework was there. I had all the doors and windows in the right rooms, but they were always locked. No one could get in, and I could not get out. I had learned how to look ok. I had learned how to protect my insides, but my protection had become my safe house. In order to use the safe house in the true essence of a safe house, I had to reestablish my boundaries. I certainly needed the boundaries to keep me safe, but I did not need to allow them to keep me from experiencing all that life has to offer. So I gave myself space; the room to mourn the losses and permission to receive the gains.

I began slowly peeling off the layers. Unmasking, I had decided to be who I am. I enjoy sharing my life with people with integrity, a desire to serve from a place of healing, and a moral compass. In the past, I had to mask UP and entertain meaningless conversations to fit in. However, with my intentional choice to unmask, I had to relearn that I was not responsible for emotionally disarming individuals and talking more than I wanted to please others, in turn giving me social jetlag and leaving me feeling depleted. I didn't force myself to be the solution. It immensely helped me in every area of life, including my practice.

I experienced an *identity shift.* I began carrying an unyielding strength, a toughness developed as a shield against life's adversities. My career demanded resilience, my relationships required endurance, and my pride in being unbreakable no longer served me. If you are like me, you may have – a yearning for a different way of being. This section reflects on my life patterns that required adjustment. I made a courageous decision to shift from *toxic strength* to *healthy vulnerability*. *"I'm fussy about me."* I discovered the *beauty of balance*. Strength wasn't about shutting off emotions; it was about navigating them with grace. Vulnerability wasn't synonymous with weakness; it was the gateway to resilience and profound connection.

I started my *Epiphany to Pink* by taking my power back. All the things I starved myself of, I now allowed myself to be and have.
I began re-evaluating my boundaries and developed my mantra: *"I'm fussy about me."* The mantra represents an intentional plan and particular standard—a set of boundaries that honor vulnerability and release toxic strength. My answer led me to become more self-aware than I had ever been. I started by exploring self-respect and empowerment to honor my needs, values, and priorities. They provide a framework for asserting my identity and maintaining a strong sense of self. *"I'm fussy about me"* was an "I said what I said" approach; I took it on with a smile and shoulders back.

Go DEEPER:

I encourage you to ask yourself questions to understand grief boundaries better, and I invite you to jot down your initial thoughts and feelings in response to these questions. Please allow your responses to be a personal reflection, an opportunity for you to connect with your emotions and begin understanding how grief boundaries may resonate with your unique journey.

What initial thoughts and feelings arise when you consider giving yourself the grace to mourn?

_____

_____

_____

_____

_____

_____

_____

_____

How might these boundaries contribute to your healing?

_____

_____

_____

_____

_____

_____

_____

What have you seen, heard, or experienced that leaves you aimlessly existing?

_____

_____

_____

_____

_____

_____

_____

_____

_____

_____

_____

_____

"I Am Fussy About Me!"

Are you ready to pledge that you will change your life? Repeat after me:

"I promise to love and respect all the parts of me,

even the ones I am still working on.

I pledge to take my time with myself while

learning, healing, and growing.

I know that I am rewritten.

I know now that I am loved; I realize I am protected. I am favored.

I pledge to implement this epiphany to pink in my daily practices.

I PLEDGE TO BE A CHAIN BREAKER".

The Professional Winner

Bree Reid

On a cool Friday night in the fall of 2018, I woke up at exactly 3:33 a.m. gasping for air. Eyes wide in search of danger, my heart pounding from fear, drenched in a night sweat, holding my chest, and coughing trying to find my normal breathing. I felt as if an unknown force had just been pulled from underwater. I lost all my breath and strength in what felt like an eternity. I was stuck in a dream. I was fighting for my life, to save myself, to see the sun again. My breaths came in quick, shallow gasps, my strength seemed weakened as I frantically whaled in fear of the unknown. This state of breathless fear would have a hold of me forever. I had no control over this situation. I was drowning. I was dying. There was a moment I felt like I needed to stop fighting and surrender to the water. Once I made that decision, I instantly found peace. I felt relaxed, unbothered, unworried, and lightweight. The sun's warmth through the water was the most pulling energy I have ever experienced. It felt comfortable, safe, and gentle, yet it moved faster than anything this Earth has ever encountered, or any human could survive. I had no idea where I was going, but I knew it was a place of Ultimate Greatness. Then I was back. Back in the room, I have been in for twenty years. As I dramatically woke from this dream, I gasped for air as if I was holding my breath in the physical world. I felt angry at that moment because the first thought that came to me was, "I'm still here?" Here in this same room, in the same city, doing the same thing, with the same people. I sat up, wondering, "what is this all about? And "what did I just experience?" An overwhelming feeling of waiting consumed me. Waiting for what or for whom, I was very unsure. However, I remained quiet and still, gathered myself, and let my breathing and heart rate return to its normal pace. My mind slowed and the fear dissipated. Randomly, I screamed out, "New York"! My face scrunched up from the unarranged blurt. Okay, now I am really confused. I have never been to New York in my life. I began to have a further conversation with myself at this moment. "What is in New York?" "Why would I go there?" My inner voice said, "You will go there to be a model." Now I am shaken because I quit modeling for at least a year and was not planning to go back to it for several reasons. Becoming a supermodel has always been my biggest dream since I was eight years old. Walking the major runways for top designers, traveling to and from the most beautiful countries in the world, and having my face on the biggest and highest magazines and billboards the world has to offer. I had big dreams, but then I got older and let society and toxic boyfriends get in my head. The dream was dead and I was on another path that I now know was not for me.

This conversation I was having with myself did not feel like I had a choice. It was not a request. It was a demand! A demand to go to New York and be a supermodel. I flopped back into my pillows and whispered to myself, "If I do not make it as a model in New York, then I must find another career." I did not sleep for the rest of the night. I stayed up and planned my exit from work, calculated my bank accounts, found somewhere to live, listed over 30 model agencies in a fifty-mile radius of New York City, and figured out how to tell my family that I was moving to New York. A week later, I quit my job working for a logistics company as a dispatcher, took all the money out of my bank accounts, and told my mother I was leaving. My mother, a New York native, expressed her fears for me, her suburban-raised child was moving to the concrete jungle. However, as a naturally supportive parent, she helped me prepare for my journey. She had no idea why I was doing this and did not press me to understand. She just knew that I was serious and needed to do this. Thankfully, she paid for my apartment for a month, and I was able to secure my living arrangements. That same day I purchased a one-way ticket to New York City. This was it! I am really doing this. I did not feel scared or nervous, even though I had never traveled alone before. I felt ready and protected. I packed two giant suitcases. One full of clothes and the other full of fur coats and shoes. I packed my whole damn closet because I knew I could not go to the fashion capital without "FLYEST" outfits.

I landed in New York on September 15, 2018. It was cold, wet, and stank. A rat as big as an alley cat scurried across my feet and I was instantly ready to go back home. I was not impressed when I walked out to smell the NYC air, but I just reminded myself why I am here and ordered myself an Uber to my new Manhattan apartment. All the bright lights, tall buildings, chilly air, and big dreams instantly brought me life and I felt ready to take on the world. I felt like the eight-year-old Bree was satisfied and excited. When I arrived at my apartment building, I again was not impressed. New York just gave me grungy, smelly, and old. "Why all the hype for this place?", I thought. I walked up to the glass door of my apartment building, put my key in the lock and found my way down an old but lit hallway, leading to an squeaky elevator. I took the elevator to the fourth floor. Stumbled to door number 403. I heard loud laughter and smelled a strong scent of Mary. I softly knocked on the door and a beautiful deep melanated girl, about my age, opened the door. She had an African accent. I asked her where she was from and she said, "Sudan". I was hypnotized by her beauty and was instantly intrigued by her and wanted to know her story. As I found my way to my room, I saw four other beautiful girls sitting in the lounging area of the box apartment. They all said hello with four different accents. Overly smiling like a weirdo, I said "wooooow" out loud. I could not believe how beautiful and foreign everyone was. I said, "hello" in my Southern American accent and claimed the last bed in the house. I happen to have found myself in a model house right after New York Fashion Week. All of the girls had just walked for the world's top French and American designers. I felt small being in the room with them because I was a girl with little to no high fashion experience. I was a newbie and in New York for the first time with a list of model agencies in my back pocket. I asked myself, "how did I get here?" The advert for the apartment said nothing about being a model house. The big voice in my head spoke and said, "You belong here. Now learn something new." I took a breather and sat with the girls; told them everything about my American life. They were just as intrigued by me as I was of them. We were all from different countries. One girl was from Brazil, another from Italy, one from Hong Kong, one from London, and the girl who answered the door from Sudan. We were all so uniquely different, but we all had the dream of being supermodels. We stayed up all night talking about life, love, and our careers and cultures. It was incredible learning about people from so many different parts of the world all at once. An experience I will never forget.

Going from a spacious four-bedroom house and private bathroom to a living room size apartment with five girls was also an experience I will never forget. Well, really six including myself. All sharing one bathroom was quite the nightmare. I thought it was bad sharing a bathroom with my two older sisters: not even close. My first night in New York was pleasant though. When I woke up the next morning, I was excited to go to my first casting at Elite Model Management. I took an Uber to the casting call because I knew trying to ride the train would be a hassle and I would end up really far and lost from where I needed to be, so I got dressed in my model attire, which was a pair of light washed Levi jeans, white tank top, black leather jacket with a pair of all white high top converse. My hair was braided in individuals and pulled up in a high ponytail. I looked like a supermodel. I felt like a supermodel. I got to the casting 15 minutes early. There is a long line outside the office door, and everyone is wearing all Black. "Damn, did I miss the dress code memo?"

I softly whispered to myself. I go into a silent panic and begin psyching myself out because I know better and should always double check things. So now I am the oddball and seen as someone who does not follow instructions. As bad as I wanted to leave, I just walked to the back of the line and did not make eye contact with anyone. When the casting call started, I prayed so hard to have high energy and for the agents to see my potential. I went in there and really gave them Bree! The big bright smile, the bubbly personality, and the long-legged stride. I saw no other way but to just be me. They decided not to sign me and I went on my way. I have twenty-nine other agencies to go to, so I was not too disappointed. Now, let us fast forward thirty days. I went to every single model agency, model audition, and casting call on my list. Not one call back! Not one agency or production company contacted me back. I cried like a baby for a week. I could not understand why I was not chosen. I have the face, the body, the personality, the talent. I am fun, cool, funny as hell, and teachable. Why not me? My attributes are literally carved in the form of a supermodel. How could they not see that? Sulking in my sorrows, I just stayed in my bed. I did not want to do anything, talk to anyone, or go anywhere. I wanted to go home and hug my momma and talk with my sisters. I was out of money at that point. I thought about getting a job and starting a life in New York, but my spirit said it was time to go home and that is exactly what I did. That was after I partied with my new model friends for two weeks straight. They told me I was not going back home without experiencing the New York nightlife. The girls taught me how to ride the train, showed me which Bodega to shop, how to hail a taxi, and took me to The Met Fifth Avenue because they knew I enjoy world history. Once I had my fun, I bought the dreaded one-way ticket back to

Atlanta with my last dollar. I went home with my first "L" Shaped trophy, but I did not feel as bad as I did when it all went down. I felt proud for stepping out of my comfort zone and doing something I thought I would never do. On the flight back home, I sat in silence with myself to process my whole experience in New York. In that silence, God spoke to me. God explained to me the purpose of going to New York. The purpose of New York was to prove to myself that I am good enough, have enough, and protected enough to do new things on my own. New York showed me that when I am obedient to God's word, I will receive everything I need. New York showed me that I am more than just being a model. My talents, my personality, and my creativity would never be appreciated as a walking hanger. New York showed me that I need to dive deeper into my spiritual body and surrender my life to God. Doing this molded me into what I call, "the professional winner". When a human is supported by The Higher Power their capability, belief, and destiny become aligned with greatness. Everything in them, on them, and around them becomes blessed.

"Trust in the Lord with all your heart and lean not on your own understanding; in all your ways submit to him, and he will make your path straight." Proverbs 3-5

A professional winner is an individual who has an endless desire to improve. From my father, I learned a word that encapsulates this definition as Arete. Arete is a concept popularized by the Greeks and is defined as "excellence," "fulfillment," or "virtue." Professional winners embrace this concept, and its traits, which manifest into self-growth. Psychologically intact humans, typically, have a greater understanding and acceptance of life and that life can and will present mistakes that manifest from their best decisions during a particular time, we fall and we sometimes fail. However, The Professional Winner is one who can stand, learns the lesson of this decision and decides to accept the challenge(s) presented. Becoming a professional winner consists of a mindset change, particularly after our decisions led to unwanted outcomes. I have learned to name the individual trials and tribulations that I experience so that I always know them when I see them. I call them "L" shaped trophies. These "L" shaped trophies must be displayed, honored, and respected by you. This is part of the mindset change required by Professional Winners.

The "L" represents three separate characteristics that remain at the forefront of a Professional Winner's thought, especially during life's difficult moments. The first of the three characteristics is Levels. Levels represent progress. This progress equates to advances in your mind, body, and spirit, on your life path, workplace responsibilities, family dynamics, or in any other areas that you deem important.

The second "L" represents the acceptance of our Losses. The method to losing is understanding and accepting that it was just not our winning moment. Many of the great historical leaders of the world have experienced many losses in the pursuit of their dreams and daily lives. Their perceived losses in any particular situation manifested a change in thought that created alternatives in behavior, which led to greater probabilities of winning, in the same or new endeavor(s).

The final "L" represents the Lesson. You must know that making mistakes in life, in business, or in general, is inevitable. There is no running from it, no hiding from it, no stashing it away somewhere, and no giving it to someone else to keep. You must put it in your pocket and carry it with you everywhere you go. There is no need for shame. That is a heavy emotion, whose only job is to bring you down. Accept your lessons because they are yours to keep and only the smart ones take them out to review sometimes as reminders to never do or let it happen again.

You are human in this realm. You are born to make mistakes. Just take accountability and learn from them. Do not make the same mistake twice.

"L" shaped trophies are gifts and must never be ignored. They are there to remind you that you are not and will not be perfect and that is okay! Being perfect is not fun nor relatable. Being perfect means, you will constantly worry about what people think of you and that will cause you to be something you are not, which will be unauthentic and unrelatable. You will mentally, physically, and spiritually die from trying to be something you are not.

To be a professional winner requires accountability, awareness, and authenticity. There is no path over or under these values. It is only through, and it is going to hurt. Do not be afraid of the pain if you want to play. The pain is your only entry into greatness. You will grow the armor that is needed for this path as you take the journey. The relationship that will be created with yourself and God will come, and you will receive all the answers, guidance, protection, and help that is needed for you to succeed. The only way to do this is to intentionally love yourself, reflect on yourself and know that you can walk the journey alone. God will send you the right people to strengthen the pathway, block the enemy, hand you food and water, shelter you when storms come, and even inspire you to continue to shine bright in your calling.

A Professional Winner does not lie to themselves. If you are someone who says you are going to do something, but consciously decides to not do it, then you are going to have a hard and long journey. Lying to yourself means that you ignore your true thoughts, real feelings, and core values. This is what I would call your intuition, which is an internal safety tool. It is not tangible. It is only a feeling. A feeling only you can sense. Ignoring this feeling can place you in situations you do not want to be in. Have you ever had a feeling where you should not do something? Or go somewhere? Or say something? That is a warning, and you should listen to it. Our bodies tend to tell us what it needs to survive. If you are hungry, tired, sore, or in pain. We have that feeling and we take action to balance things out. Intuition is no different and should not be ignored.

Lying to yourself means you find excuses to not do what really needs to be done. To be a professional winner there is no easy path, there are no shortcuts, there is no long-lasting comfort zone. I am going to be transparent with you. On the path of becoming a professional winner there is constant pressure, body aches, sleep deprivation, loneliness, self-doubt, worry, and anxiety. The journey is about overcoming your fears, taking the lead of your own life, and knowing you are enough. You must love what you are doing or else none of this will be fun. You will have to do things that scare you. Things that scare you, so much that you shake in your skin, jump out your boots, or even run away. There is a quote said by Ellen Johnson Sirleaf, who was the first woman to be elected head of state of Liberia from 2006 to 2018. She said, "if your dreams don't scare you, they are not big enough." That quote has stuck with me for six years now. I have been scared for a long time, but I demand to keep pushing because I desire to inspire the masses with confidence and courage to authentically be themselves. To be a professional winner requires commitment, an open mind, and a splash of arrogance. You must set goals and take action. You must actively listen and receive information. You must know that you belong in the room and never dim your light to bring comfort to others.

Follow the Path of a Professional W.I.N.N.E.R.

Wait—Having the ability to be patient is a major aspect to becoming a professional winner. You must have moments to observe your environment. It does not matter if you have been there a million times or freshly off a plane. You must feel the energy where you stand because one day it can change, and you must be aware of it. Having patience keeps you on your toes. Use your physical and spiritual senses to analyze the room, the people, the field, and the vibe. The waiting stage is always first Ie this Is where you do your visual research. It requires you to investigate body language, actively listen, instead of being heard or seen. This might be difficult for some of you. It sure was for me because I thrive in the spotlight, however I learned the hard way – that you will learn further in this chapter – that having patience, being quiet and observant will save your life, promote you to your dream job, or give you

DEEPER Women™ TEACH: Volume 3

the upper hand in tricky situations. People are so distracted; they will not even notice that they are exposing themselves to a dynamic individual like yourself. They will underestimate you, but you will use that to your advantage because when it is your time to be seen, you will be prepared to perform. Mouths will drop, eyebrows will rise and now you are on the map. The power of patience is peculiar for most but prominent to you. Being quiet helps you stay focused on your goals. Patience gives you strength because all you are doing in this moment of silence is receiving. Receiving information that will scale you, shield you, strengthen you, and even save you. This is how you start your process of becoming a professional winner.

Internalize—A professional winner is someone who knows themselves. Someone who practices diving deeper into their mind. Doing this guides you to your truth, your purpose, and your individual power. To dig deeper into yourself you must have conversations with yourself about your day, the people you interacted with, the emotions you felt and situations you may have experienced that day. You are what you attract, so analyze the things that are around you. Do not ask yourself why questions, such as "why is this happening to me." Ask yourself questions that help you think about your emotions such as, "how does this make me feel," "Can I or should I remove myself?" This is the stage where you set boundaries and standards. This is the pushy stage because setting boundaries and standards will push several people away. It will push people you thought were solid in your circle. This is an incredibly challenging stage, and most individuals will give up here because it takes consistent judgment of yourself and that can be physically, mentally, and spiritually painful. It is the stage of losing and gaining. It is the rebirth stage; the level of reimagining yourself. I personally lost a lot of sleep here; however, I knew I had to keep going because I really wanted to love myself. You cannot fear your truth or find excuses to not take accountability for the choices you make. Be persistent with your standards and boundaries. Respect them, support them and keep your word. If you decide on something, then stick with it. Do not tell yourself to do something and you completely bail on it. If you lie to yourself, then you will forever be in a cycle of self-deception. Humans are masters at self-deception. We fool ourselves into believing things that are false and refuse to believe things that are true. We lie to ourselves because we do not have enough psychological strength to admit the truth and deal with the consequences that will follow. When we admit who we really are, we can change. Opportunity represents choice. When we do not take full responsibility for who we are, we hurt ourselves and everyone around us. How do we start acknowledging the lies we tell ourselves? In my five years of awareness, I have come to find two ways to answer this question. First, being self-aware. Become an observer of yourself. For example, when you have a strong emotional reaction to something, give yourself a moment to stop and think about how you are about to respond. Is the person or situation worth the energy you are about to throw at it? When what you say does not match how you act; what does that say about you? The more aware you become the more responsible you are about your choices. Either do something about it or not. People become afraid or lazy of this responsibility, which is a shame because they now know better but still decide to be a loser. The truth, The pain, The struggle is truly a gift if you are courageous enough to accept it. Second, choose to become more honest about the lies you tell yourself. This is an ongoing challenge and

Network—Networking involves creating links and fostering relationships with others. These connections can offer valuable guidance, introductions, and opportunities that can shape your life choices. Networking can also aid in discovering unmarked job or internship openings. It can occur in both group settings and individual interactions. A professional winner is intentional with the people they meet. When you know what you want but have no idea how you are going to get it done, you find the resources of people to help you make it happen. A professional winner is nothing without support. You need people to do business, build a brand, climb to the next level, and even watch your back. If you do not have a network, then you have nothing. Support is a requirement because there will be times when you will convince yourself to quit and move on to something less complicated. The people around you who see your hard work, your drive and consistency will naturally encourage you and even help you build your confidence back up and you can continue your journey. These are the people you keep around to maintain a balanced mindset.

Navigate—When you have an idea and set goals to activate your ideas, you will know an opportunity when you see one. As a professional winner you are constantly studying your environment, your industry, yourself. It becomes a sixth sense after practicing and experiencing the first two stages for a while. Movement is survival in this stage. You must have three to four reasons why you decide to move towards something. If you are not receiving at least two of those reasons, move on to something more relevant and beneficial to your life. This type of awareness will prevent your time from being wasted, money from being spent on irrelevant materials, and your passion from being pushed to the back of your mind. A professional winner mentally develops what I call the Bee Es sensor in this stage. You will have the ability to detect and respond to nonsense, lies and exaggerations of people, contracts, imagery, etc. You learn this by continuously studying body language, reading, and meditation.

Emotional Intelligence—Having emotional intelligence takes several decades to master. It takes embarrassment and exposure to develop. It also takes accountability, self-control, self-awareness, sacrifice, and accepting people where they are in life. Developing emotional intelligence will be one of the hardest things you will experience as a human. We are all drenched in emotions and have the willpower to express them. The intelligence part is knowing when and which emotion to express in all situations and conversations.

Risk Taker – To be a professional winner taking risk is your fuel. You must be comfortable with being uncomfortable. What are some of your most comfortable spaces to be in? Like me, say if the shower is your happy place. It is warm, steamy, and refreshing. Now imagine that warm and steamy place becoming ice cold and slippery. That is life as a professional winner. If that is something you are not willing to do, then now you know that this is not your path and that is okay. You are still good enough to make life abundantly beautiful for yourself. In order to achieve a goal, you must do something that feels a little dangerous or scary. A professional winner is comfortable with being uncomfortable.

They are willing to adjust and adapt to their environment as situations arise. To be a consistent risk taker you must have intention. You must have a reason why you are doing what you are doing. If you do not know the reason you are doing something, then you are being reckless and irresponsible, which can be a risk to your life.

The H.E.A.L.I.N.G. Journey

Dearice Spencer-Shackleford

I keep hearing his voice." Babe, I'm sorry. I know it hurts. Please forgive me!" Tears are flowing profusely. I keep hyperventilating as I stand in the dark, facing the hinges of my bathroom door. I call out to God. " God, please help me; I think I'm going crazy." I keep hearing his voice, knowing he's gone!

I dreaded the day of even thinking about this, let alone writing about it. I knew it would bring up more than just feelings of missing my husband; it would also bring up the emotional outburst that comes with it. But think about it: this experience almost took me out. I've been through some humdingers, but this, losing my Dad and my husband, truly and honestly, broke my heart. Let me not jump ahead; there's so much more to my story than just heartbreak. Join me as I share my **H.E.A.L.I.N.G.** journey.

What do you do when the love of your life passes away? Hmm, and your father, too? You know what I did? I silently had a nervous breakdown. I became suicidal and depressed, begging God to take me in my sleep while I slept on the floor every night, unable to sleep in our bed. I often clenched my chest from the enormous, overwhelming feeling of a broken heart. It is true what they say. You can die from a broken heart. I felt myself slowly drifting away after experiencing this loss. I wanted to and even welcomed my exit as I cried myself to sleep at night. No one could've prepared me for this. I'd just graduated from college, a fifteen-year-old dream finally accomplished, and I was currently employed at a Psych hospital working in my field. I was finally on top. My life had finally gotten on course. Or so I thought.

At the time, I lived without a cell phone, liberated from a device and bill I didn't need. I sat at a desk where my phone rang nonstop for twelve hours of the day, so I did not need a cell phone. My house phone was for the children to contact me after school and while I was at work. After a long day of work in December 2017, my mother walked into my room and handed me her cell phone, and the voice on the other end informed me that my father had passed away. Unnoticed, I dropped the phone as I began to scream aloud and cry out as I fell to the floor. I was devastated by this news; I never thought this would happen. My father was one of the healthiest men I knew physically. He was a martial arts expert. He never smoked, drank, or used any drugs. To my mind, this made no sense. When I gathered myself, the next thought was, "How will I get myself and three children from Texas to Brooklyn, New York?"

I wish I could tell you the backstory of my life with my father. I could tell you it was filled with days at the park and private karate instructions or that he would spend hours imparting fatherly wisdom into his doting daughter's mind. That would be so far from the truth. Our relationship was diminished to weekends and some visits to my paternal grandparents' house. But I did love and worship my father and see him as the black Bruce LeRoy. All these childhood thoughts flooded my mind as I would never see my father again or have an adult relationship with the man who will always be my hero. Now, I had to tell my employer, where I had just started working in October, that I needed a week off to bury my father in Brooklyn, New York. I was holding it together as best I could but never prepared for what would happen next. I am grateful for my supervisor, co-workers, and peers at my job. They donated funds for me and my children so we could rent a car and go to my father's funeral. God always seems to work things out, doesn't He?

I rented a car, packed up my children and myself, and hit the highway straight northeast on Interstate 30 on my way to New York. I left on a Thursday afternoon, mentally determined to embark on this solo drive home to Brooklyn. I drove all night without any breaks until I made it to Pennsylvania. I had no more left in me. I had to shut my eyes for at least an hour. While driving, I had multiple moments of tearful steering during my alone time. Conversations with God, asking for protection as I drove 90 to 100 mph. And other times, asking why things had to end like this without closure. Many questions about what happened and why flooded my mind while driving. I arrived in Brooklyn that Saturday morning, December 23, 2017. Just in time for the services, unable to change or freshen up. I had to attend the service in the clothes I drove in on Thursday. But I made it.

You're probably wondering, well, that seems like a pretty nice ending to this story, right? But wait, there's so much more. While home in Brooklyn, I made it my mission to discover what happened to my father. This would resemble the first stage of grief, shock, and disbelief. Back then, I'd handle things from a" rush in guns blazing" approach to prove my point. I was determined to get to the bottom of my father's passing and get some answers. My Daddy wound demanded that I prove my loyalty and love. Being the eldest, it was expected of me. It never crossed my mind to carve out time to mourn for my father or address my abandonment issue of him not being around. Never did this process cross my mind. I've been traveling between Brooklyn, NY, and Orange, NJ, to spend time with my husband. Who, as newlyweds, were going through our trials and tribulations.

My husband and I lived in two separate locations. As stated earlier, I lived in Texas, and my husband resided in New Jersey. Our relocation plans were on hold due to my son's last year in high school. Navigating a new marriage, a teenage son and the passing of my father was, for sure, a divine journey of healing. This journey was unfathomable to me. To add to the backstory, my husband is a marine vet who served in Iraq. He was doing his best to cope with his experience of healing mentally and emotionally. It's amazing when God chooses you to embark on a journey to transform your life; it never makes sense or feels good.

Being "superwoman", I attempted to be, I began to run myself back and forth from my husband's apartment to all my family's homes in Brooklyn. I couldn't harness my thoughts or emotions. I was constantly moving, addressing everything. I was numb to all of it, just smiling and self-medicating with marijuana. I solely depended on my husband for moral support and comfort. I only mourned for my father around my husband. He was the only person I allowed myself to be vulnerable with. He became my rock, my safe space. I was usually the strong one in our union, taking on the role of counselor and therapist. But honestly, I was broken inside. My father was gone. The little girl inside never understood why she lost him twice.

While traveling between NJ and NY, my husband and I wanted to live with him in New Jersey. I never took the time to evaluate my environment while in NJ or NY. I dreaded the day when we'd have to travel back to Texas. I was in the early stages of grief and never acknowledged any part of it. I'd been wearing rose-colored glasses the entire duration of my trip while constantly ignoring my thoughts and emotions. I was not focused on the things around me and left unaddressed issues in the air. This made for a bumpy journey leaving the East Coast. Nothing had been resolved between my husband and me. The night before we left, an argument ensued, leaving two hotheads angry that they were parting ways to live a plan they both agreed upon. We both hated being apart from one another, and I regretted leaving my husband on January 3, 2018, at 1 am due to ego and immaturity.

We arrived in Texarkana on January 5, 2018; I cried all the way home while everyone slept. I was constantly repeating arguments and scenarios in my head. I had no idea how to create a positive narrative during this season of my life, yet I kept going. My main concern when I pulled into the driveway was, " I've got to get this car clean, fueled, and returned by the set time." I knew this week would be hectic, and there was no time to catch my breath. I had taken an extra week while in Brooklyn because my children's aunt had passed away while we were there. Considering my circumstances, I had children to attend to, not to mention my job, which was being so lenient towards me. I was just grateful to have a career in my field of study; I knew this was very rare, considering I had just graduated and received my degree.

Monday morning came, and nothing unusual occurred during the start of my day. I got the children off to school and myself to work. While driving to work, I had my regular call with my husband. This is routine for our day as we return to our "normal." As the week went on, we continued with the regular after-work call until Wednesday. On Wednesday, the flow of the conversations was a bit off. My husband was a United States Marine Veteran, and sometimes his conversation ould a little bizarre. But this time, looking back, it seemed to foretell what was coming, but because we were talking and not arguing, I ignored the warnings and reveled in the land of blissfulness.

There were so many statements like, "You know I love you, right?' "No matter what anybody says, okay?" He kept this saying repeatedly. My response was the same every time. I tried changing the subject multiple times, talking about the children and how excited they are to move up north in May. He kept circling back to the previous statement. 'You know I love you, right?" " No matter what anyone says, okay?" And he adds the nail in the coffin. "I love you, Reesie Cup!" At that moment, I stopped what I was doing and then asked. " What's wrong? Are we getting a divorce?" He laughs and replies, " No, girl, do you think I'd divorce you." "I love you too much." Immediately, I knew in my spirit something was wrong, and he was keeping something from me. I just couldn't put my finger on it. All day, I heard the same phrase from him. I wasn't that delusional anymore. I felt something that I just couldn't shake. As a veteran's wife of someone who had fought in a war, I'd experienced him on his low days. You become familiar with the jargon, but this was different. Yes, I have gotten those calls about committing suicide from him before. However, we agreed he would continue going to the VA hospital for help.

Wednesday night, after a work call, his speech was slightly slurred. My husband drank when he felt low. I knew this and governed myself accordingly. I knew when to tread lightly with the conversations and which topics to embark upon. I knew what I signed up for concerning him. January 9, 2018, at 10 pm CST will always be a date embedded in my mind. This was the last time I spoke with my husband. My husband's last words were, "I love you, Reesie Cup. Remember that, no matter what people say, okay?" "I'mma call you back."

I woke up Thursday morning and nothing. I had been calling all morning while getting ready for work, leaving message after message on his voicemail. I thought, "Well, maybe his phone is dead, and he is still asleep." I kept trying to reach him via phone, but still nothing.

Friday morning, I am still waiting to hear from him. I began to leave messages that were filled with multiple emotions. Some were filled with anger, others with sheer confusion from not knowing what was going on. My emotions were all over the place; I couldn't even think straight at this point. The children kept asking me if I had heard from him. My son was calling him on his phone and couldn't get to him either. He left a message. I began to think he was on another low and didn't want to talk to me when he was like that, but internally, I knew it was so much more. Being in such a fragile state of mind and lacking emotional intelligence, there was no stopping me from going down the rabbit hole of my thoughts. I knew something was wrong. Friday evening comes, and still no word from my husband. We've never gone this long without hearing from each other. I couldn't sleep all night, wondering what was happening with my husband. I kept asking God what was going on.

Saturday morning greets me with a small voice telling me to sign into Facebook and look on mutual people's pages that we both knew. That's right, folks, I found out my husband had passed away from social media. Someone had posted a picture of him with the caption, "Who loved you more, Bruh? Only God knows. This one hurts. God, I miss you, Earl!" I couldn't and wouldn't believe it. I went to different people's pages, and his face was everywhere. I started screaming, saying, "No, no, no, this can't be. My husband is dead, Earl is dead." My cousin, who came back to Texas with me from Brooklyn, took the phone from me to see what I was looking at. I couldn't believe it; just four days ago, we were talking on the phone—the overflow of loving bliss and admiration towards one another. I knew something was not right.

This was the beginning of my emotional and mental descent into the black hole of depression. Honestly, I cannot recall my actions during this time. I lived on autopilot. I cried nonstop–begging God to take me in my sleep. I arose daily, continuing my morning routines, waking the children, and getting them off to school, all while not eating or bathing. Thank God I wore an afro, which is the most effortless style for me. All I had to do was pull my hair back into a puff. My countenance was gray because that's exactly how I felt–numb, lost, and filled with regrets about returning to Texas.

I cried so much; surprised I never ran out of tears. I slept on my bedroom floor because sleeping in the bed was not an option. I saw my husband's face everywhere I turned, and his smell seemed to be everywhere. We spent time at each other's homes occasionally, and memories began to flood my mind of our quality time together. Isn't it funny how good memories flood your head when a loved one transitions? All the memories of happy times shared and regrets of not spending more time with that individual play on repeat. I wanted more time, good, bad, or ugly. I wanted more time.

Immediately, I was thrust into the stages of grief. I began to blame myself for not being there when my husband needed me or when he closed his eyes. I continued to sink lower and lower into depression and guilt and physically experienced the effects of a broken heart. You know you can die from a broken heart, and I welcomed it, wanted it. Every day, I felt my heart break more and more. How do you get out of this dark place? I became an empty shell of myself. I constantly heard my husband's voice whenever I cried. " Babe, I'm sorry. I didn't mean to hurt you." Crying became the main activity of my day. I cried myself to sleep. I cried when getting dressed for work. I cried in between the intake patients. I cried after every phone call I answered. I cried whenever I saw a couple, a family, or a husband anywhere I went. Crying had become my best friend.

One night, I had a nervous breakdown. I began to hyperventilate, so I ran into my bathroom. It was late at night, and I didn't want to wake anyone in the house. I kept the light off, closed the door, and then faced the hinges of the door. Unable to catch my breath or stop crying, I called out to God. "Please, help me, God. I feel like I'm going crazy because I keep hearing him. Please, help me, God". During this episode, I could hear my husband's voice saying, "I'm so sorry, babe. God, please help her. She won't stop crying".

Immediately, I felt the arms of God wrap around me and hold me. Instantly, my breathing began to regulate itself, and I stopped crying. I walked over to the sink, turned on the light, and finally looked at myself in the mirror. I said aloud, "I don't know why we went through this, but we're still here, so it must be for a reason." At that moment, God said, "Your life will be a testimony for others to see how you made it through this, and I will teach you how you will do it. I will teach you how to heal without prescriptions or weed". Yes, you read that right. I needed something to help me cope. I didn't drink alcohol, so I made do. I wasn't completely delivered from my vices.

I didn't understand then, but now I know why God had to take me through this process to break me and prepare me for this very moment.

I couldn't understand it then, but I do now. From that encounter with God, everything changed. God began to give me small steps to follow and add to my morning routine. By this time, I was no longer working in corporate America. God gave me the luxury of free time.

The process started so gently. First, God began showing me how my thoughts affected my emotions. When I woke up in the morning, lying in bed, I would reminisce about my husband. Right before guilt or any negative thought would form, what seemed like a play would echo in my mind.

God: What are you thinking about?"
Me: Earl.

God: What about him are you thinking and feeling?
Me: How much I miss him and love him.

God: Good, now go write that down. What you're thinking and feeling. Control your thoughts; don't let them control you.

With God's guidance, I started creating the steps to a H.E.A.L.I.N.G. journey. I embarked on the evolution of releasing grief and healing from loss. Everywhere I turned, God gave me instructions on how to take notes. I couldn't go anywhere without a notebook and pen. The process started to formulate right before my very eyes—the natural way to heal from trauma and release grief.

Harness your thoughts—Healing requires you to HARNESS YOUR THOUGHTS. Our mind is so powerful that it can either make or break us, but we also have the power to control it. When you are in a challenging phase in your life, you usually think negatively, but this time, try redirecting your thoughts to something positive.

Evaluate your environment—Healing will need an evaluation of your environment. You need to look around and ask yourself these questions:

- Where are you?
- What is the conversation in your atmosphere?
- Who's speaking to you about what's going on in your life?
- Are you in a peaceful place?

If you are not in a quiet place, you must relocate yourself. You need to remove yourself from that situation. Sometimes, you must eliminate the things that remind you of the problem. You may have to throw away things and cleanse your space/environment of triggers that remind you of what hurt you.

Affirm with positive self-talk—Communicate with yourself better and be more considerate. When you make a mistake instead of saying harsh or harmful words towards yourself, like "I'm so stupid, I'm so dumb."
You have to change your self-talk. You have to affirm yourself.
Say things like

- "I am courageous for taking on this challenge,"
- "I made a mistake, but that means I'm getting closer to figuring it out,"
- "I'm so proud of me!"

Learn from your past and re-strategize—In most instances, we repeat our past when we haven't learned a particular lesson from an occurrence in our lives. Today, I encourage you to give yourself grace and remember a similar experience. Take a survey of the circumstances of the past. Ask yourself the following questions:

- What is happening?
- Why is it happening?
- How did I react to it before?
- Can I change it now?

By taking a step back and gaining a different perspective of your past, you can devise a different way to maneuver on your journey.

Initiate a new plan—Healing is challenging. To avoid returning to what has hurt you, INITIATE A NEW PLAN. You need a new plan to see new results. Yes, it's challenging, but because it is difficult, choose to challenge yourself. No one ever completed a task without experiencing challenges.

Navigate through your obstacles—Healing will require you to navigate through your obstacles. Identify your obstacles and navigate through them rather than around them. Face them head-on, regardless of how difficult they may seem. To navigate through your obstacles, you must be all in. Make sure you protect your healing journey and set boundaries.

Gauge your progress—Feeling stuck in your HEALING JOURNEY is normal but take heart; you are slowly progressing. You can gauge your progress by asking questions like:

- How do you feel once you set these boundaries?

- How do you feel once you start your new plan?
- How do you feel now that you have cleaned your space?

As you respond to these questions, you will be surprised by your progress.

Go DEEPER:

What thoughts or feelings are you not harnessing?

_____

_____

_____

_____

_____

_____

_____

_____

_____

_____

_____

_____

_____

_____

_____

_____

_____

_____

_____

How does your environment contribute to your healing process?

_____

_____

_____

_____

_____

_____

_____

Self-talk is the inner dialogue we have with ourselves. What have you been saying to you about you? Write some self-affirming statements below.

_____

_____

_____

_____

_____

_____

_____

_____

_____

_____

_____

_____

_____

_____

What have you learned from your past experiences? How will you restrategize moving forward?

_____

_____

_____

_____

_____

_____

_____

_____

_____

_____

You need a new plan to see new results. Write a new plan below that maps out your plan to release the unhealed version of yourself.

_____

_____

_____

_____

_____

_____

_____

_____

_____

_____

_____

You will run into opposition, internally and externally. You are a natural-born problem solver. How will you address obstacles? i.e., setting boundaries, considering people's points of view, etc.

_____

_____

_____

_____

_____

_____

_____

_____

_____

_____

_____

_____

_____

_____

_____

_____

_____

_____

_____

_____

_____

_____

_____

From the Absence of Light to Illumination

Sandra Tescum

We all question our life at some point: Who am I? Am I happy? Is what I have accomplished enough? Why did I push to achieve these things? What now? Usually, this occurs when either you go through a divorce, you have suffered a loss, or you are grieving, which could be the loss of a job, loved one, pet, friend, or opportunity, or your kids are growing up and no longer need you in the capacity they did as children-This is a big one, especially for single mothers like me. Although you are now free to do anything you want (at least that's how others who are not in the situation see it), you feel trapped in a downward racing bobsled that's moving at 100 miles per hour towards your final days, sometimes feeling like it's time to plan your retirement from life. I should be providing positivity in this piece, but to truly get the message, you must see the situation or my perception of the situation first, and then we can rise from the darkness to see and feel the light. One of my favorite sayings is, 'Darkness is the absence of light'. Light and darkness have a yin and yang relationship that balances and complements each other; they are inextricably connected. My favorite definition of illumination is that it is the spiritual light that brightens your heart when you receive divine enlightenment. The most remarkable appreciation of illumination comes from experiencing the absence of light.

I am a self-diagnosed introvert and neurodivergent who chose to live and survive life by living in the shadows and the cracks. Feeling like I am hidden; the spotlight will not shine on me, and I can go through life quietly without anyone knowing of my presence, fading into the tapestry and wallpaper of life. I began asking myself those questions I opened with after I earned my master's degree, and I began to see my children, particularly, my son getting older, who soon will be on his own. He is my youngest, and once he is gone, I will be faced with my biggest fear of being alone. The oxymoron is that I enjoy being alone but not alone from the ones I love. This fear comes from when I was a tiny child, and my grandmother would leave me in the dark late at night to go to the canal in Belize to dump the waste. I know you're probably thinking- what? Yes, you read that correctly. We had no sewer system back then, so you would have to use the outhouse in a five-gallon bucket, and when it was full, you would take it to the canal and dump it- the canal stayed clean because it was filled with catfish that would enjoy the delicacies (hence why lots of older Belizeans don't see catfish). Anyway, my grandmother would leave me alone in the dark- mind you, there were no house lights, so imagine how dark that was. I would sit by the window in my little nightie, covering my legs so nothing could touch them, and I would cry from the time she headed to the gate until I could see her haloed silhouette brightening the path as she grew closer, eyes piercing to see through the extreme darkness eagerly waiting to see her flicker. The feeling of aloneness, being unprotected, would consume every inch of my little body. When she returned and we went back to bed, I would hold her tight and never let her go until morning. That was the first experience that initiated my fear of the dark and being alone.

All my achievements were not accomplished for me or because that was what I wanted personally. Subconsciously- they were to show my family that I could be and will be more than they coined me to be as a child- a burden in their eyes that would never amount to anything or achieve anything; therefore, they saw no reward in keeping or nurturing me or at least that is what I believed, but I will show them! Consciously, it was to show my children that achievement of education was the way to live the life they wanted and financially have the things they wanted without depending on others. I had learned those harsh lessons of relying on others and never wanting that for them. Those were my goals for achievement. The funny thing is now, when I look back, I cannot think of one thing I ever did or achieved for personal gratification. They were always aligned to take revenge on my family and how they looked at me as a child and to protect and give my kids everything I did not have while preparing them not to suffer my traumas.

In the last few years, as I achieved so many educational and career goals and my kids began growing further and further from me, piercing the bubble that held the four of us tightly together, my world, as I saw it, began to fall apart. The invisible bubble was slowly fading away. The positive is that it unexpectedly allowed light to shine into those shadowy areas and cracks where I lived most of my life. I began to experience my divine enlightenment, and the light revealed the true me that God had been molding like a sculpture in the darkness. I had no choice but to come out of the darkness, enter the stage, and light the path prepared for me. I now know an essential part of my mission is to unveil Sandra to the world.

From childhood to adulthood, I hated writing in school, but I stepped outside my comfort zone to bring this story and message forward; it is also a significant step in my healing. I needed to get it out and, in the process, go deeper inside of me to bring back who God intended me to be, who I am, and who the world now sees me as a leader, an inspiration to others on the same journey, a flame that emanates a flicker of hope that is just enough to see the goal, the prize, the reason to continue. Let us go hand in hand forward through this journey. I will tell you there will be rocky, winding terrain, valleys, mountains, and, at times, loss of oxygen, darkness, and then, light.

Go DEEPER:

How often are you receiving and noting what God reveals to your heart-your divine enlightenment? What do you plan to do with it?

My Journey- God Never Gives You More Than You Can Handle

I never thought that one day I would be someone who would lead and inspire others. Suppose you ask me when I was thirteen, or even when I was five, if I saw myself as a leader, a woman who inspires other women, I would say, "Hell no!" But, through God's grace and plan for me, here I am today. Many have told me that I inspire and motivate and that I am seen as a leader in my professional life. Still, I only knew what that meant for me once I took the time to go deeper and look at all the things I've accomplished through diversity. Looking back over the past 20 years and reading my resume, I was shocked. I was like, "Wow, girl, you did that! I need to meet you; you are a superhero." That's when I realized that the Chica I was talking to and wanting to meet was me. That was when I began to realize that I am a leader. I am someone who inspires. I am someone who motivates, and I'm here to share that because this is the only way I will lean into my healing and true calling and pay it forward.

When I was about 20 years old, I wondered why I was here throughout my life and struggles. Why did God put me on this earth to struggle like I did? Was I a mistake? Was I a black jellybean that was thrown into a bag of pink jellybeans and did not belong? Am I the shunned black duckling in the pond of yellow ducklings? Is that what I am? What I was? But now, as I look to the present, I realize it just took me time to figure out that I am a beautiful one-of-a-kind artwork God purposely created in the darkness. Now, I am prepared to be illuminated to emphasize and enhance my uniqueness while exposing the narrative that God, as the artist, wanted to convey. I'm so happy that I finally realized my calling, purpose, and why I survived this boot camp of life: to live and tell this story, sit in it, stand in it, heal from it, and be true to it.

"God never gives you more than you can handle." Yeah, I have been hearing that all my life, and for every challenge that I faced, it was my go-to. Whenever I reached that point where my mind and emotions made me feel like -When will it end? Should I make an executive decision to end it? That was when I knew I needed to retreat and focus on my mantra: "God never gives you more than you can handle." I say mantra because, as the definition states, it is a "sacred utterance" that was my invocation or petition to God for help, a "Hey God, yoo-hoo, over here" (waving emoji) to remind him I was here- just in case he forgot, and I was mistakenly getting more than I could handle so he could course correct. He always came through for me; however, not how I wanted him to, but in his way, according to his master plan, which I could not see then. However, he showed up, always giving me that extra boost or reminder that I needed to continue the journey, pick up my bootstraps and hoses, and keep moving.

As I got older, I became someone people would turn to for advice. My message to them would always be what I relied on to continue- my mantra. Whenever I heard the challenges that they were facing or the things that they were struggling with, I would say, "Well, God never gives you more than you can handle." Keep that in the forefront of your mind and your heart as you push through the current challenges, struggles, and difficulties affecting you.

How does that work? Well, it takes two things. You must have faith and trust in God or the higher power you believe in (whatever it or they may be called), and trust in yourself. When you trust in God, you understand that nothing is impossible, and you understand that if he has given or placed it in your life, it is for you, and there is a reason you must endeavor. One of the things that I always think about in those moments is that God believes and trusts in me, and he believes I can do it; then, I must trust him and believe I can do it and venture on. I know I have been talking a lot about God, although I have never been a super churchgoer. However, what I have built throughout my life, starting from a young teenager, is a personal relationship with God. As I got older, our relationship just got stronger. Through all my struggles, as I experienced most of them physically alone, I always felt a presence that brought me peace in the moment or helped me escape in the moment to a place of peace in my mind.

As I think back on my earliest childhood memory or my first traumatic experience in life and chronologically through all the others, I realize that there was always a silent voice, an inner light that coached me, empowered me, and pushed me when I wanted to give up. It made me start to realize that I must have a purpose here because there is no way that God doesn't like me and wants to punish me over and over and over. As a child, I felt that way, that I was being punished, and I did not understand why. But as I got older, I started to see from a higher plane and saw a different reflection of me- the way the light broke through allowed me a moment of reflection or pause amidst the chaos to return to my journey with purpose. This preparation and boot camp called "My Life" got me to this point where I can empower and inspire someone else with my story and words. Sometimes, even when I speak, I feel like it is not something I'm making up in my head but just the illumination flowing through my heart and transmuting into reachable words. I always felt like it came from God, and he gave me those words and messages because he expected me to share them.

As I started to understand my purpose and as shy as I am, the introvert that I am, the one that never wanted to be on a stage, always lurking in the corner, never wanted to be in the spotlight, never wanting people to really, truly look at me because all they saw was this beautiful face and body as they would describe it. The one that always brought me unwanted attention and got me into situations that led to experiences I chose to lock in my Pandora box and never open. They couldn't see the masterpiece God was creating- I didn't see it either back then until I realized that my true beauty and purpose sat within, and the beautiful shell people saw was just an illusion.

No Excuses- You are Worthy!

As a young adult, I was always ashamed of my story of being smuggled into the United States at the age of six or seven alone in the back of a truck, hiding underneath piles of hay and boxes and different items, just like in the movies. (Sidebar: this is my second reason for my fear of darkness and being alone) This was my first traumatic experience, and I always felt like no one truly understood what that experience was like for me, the fear and loneliness I felt on that trip. I was always ashamed that I didn't have a mother and a father to raise me because my father would not claim me as his child. My mother had so many kids that she could not financially take care of me and gave me up as a newborn, which then led to me having to experience that first childhood trauma. As I grew older, being out in the world just opened me to the elements because no one wanted me, moving from household to household; I remember being pawned off to some of my father's in-laws who wanted to adopt a girl child to give the facade of a perfect relationship with her soon to be husband. I remember spending those weekends as a servant, maid, and nanny to other in-laws, and starving during the week because I was left alone in a home without any food, being beaten with an extension cord while kneeling on a food grater because I tried to cook and burned a pot because I was starving, not sleeping at night in fear of being sexually assaulted, and then returned like a shoe that you wear a few times and decide you don't want. I remember being shipped to New York around the age of twelve (where I met my spiritual mom) and eventually ending up homeless on the streets of New York City as a teen. I remember sleeping wherever I could, which offered shelter enough for me to close my eyes for a couple of hours without being harmed. I was ashamed of my experiences of being "touched" by my supposed family member and being blamed, being sexually assaulted by an ex-convict neighbor, and physically and mentally abused by boyfriends as I got older. At times, I was ashamed of just being. I felt that how I felt about myself was how everyone else felt about me. I was a burden, a horrible stain, and an annoyance in everyone's life, like a piece of dirty paper drifting through the New York streets without a destination. Those are, I think, the critical times when I asked God, why am I here? Why am I being punished with this life? Why am I not worthy of the life I see other teenagers living?

During my period of teen homelessness, I would visit my favorite cousin every Sunday. There, I could escape for a couple of hours from my reality. My cousin and aunt were among the few people who accepted me and never judged me as the stereotype of homeless people who often are considered thieves, drug addicts, and criminals, people you do not want in your home. I was none of those, just a child without a home. They embraced me and showed me a flicker of good in people and unconditional love regardless of my circumstances. When I disappeared because of those circumstances and returned, they embraced me with hugs, never judging, never asking. I was welcomed, seen, and respected as a human being at their home; it was a momentary paradise. Their home was where I retreated after being violently sexually assaulted at 16 by an ex-convict who had just been released from jail and lived across the street from me. This criminal knew I lived alone and had no one, so he did what most predators do. After the act, I got dressed and walked to my cousin's house in pain from fighting as hard as I could and losing. I acted as if nothing was wrong and continued with life. On my walk there, I remember talking to God and asking when it would end, why he would not let me go so I could end it, and why he kept holding me in this hell called earth. I realized that God was strategically placing specific experiences and people in my life to ensure I stayed on this journey, continuing to gain the skills and earning the superpower he had for me. There was no way I could have made it this far without those strategically placed supporting characters of this story. As hard as it is for me, I share all of this to touch someone and bring a flicker of light to someone who needs it. Also, I need to release it so it no longer lives inside me.

Where I am today and the things that I have accomplished in life seem unreal. If you asked me back then if I saw myself being here, thriving and achieving, my answer would be, "Hell no, I am barely surviving." If you asked me back then, where do I see my future? I probably would have said- in the grave and, at times, feeling willingly ready to go, but again, if you go back to my mantra- God never gives you more than you can handle? I got through it. I got through the next, the next, and the next, and here I am today, sharing all of this with you all and hopefully helping you who are going through challenges and feeling like you don't know your purpose or feeling like you don't understand why God is punishing you, feeling like your life is a waste, like you have no one, feeling like no one understands what you're going through, feeling like you're the only one going through these experiences or has ever gone through these experiences, I say to you, God never gives you more than you can handle. If you have faith in God and you have faith in yourself, you can make it through, and you can make it to that future that your younger self or your current self cannot see or did not see as your future.

One thing people always say to me in my professional career is, "You have a way with people." You have this unique ability to connect with people and to empower and inspire people. I do not see it the way everyone else sees it. But I feel like I do not have to. If this is my purpose here: to touch, connect, inspire, and empower, and if I am accomplishing that, praise be to God- my light and my protection, because something had to be protecting me for me to make it here 53 years later. I am accomplishing my purpose, and that brings me satisfaction and contentment, and it brings me peace and stability. What I was missing in my past life, what I was missing in my childhood and through my journey to wholeness, was stability, love of self, and understanding of my purpose. If you have made it through the storm, pat yourself on the back, you are worthy of that. Acknowledge and be proud of yourself. It is essential to love and inspire yourself before you can love and inspire others. Like the flight attendant always says, put the oxygen mask on yourself first, then you can tend to others.

Go DEEPER:

Stability, love of self, and understanding my purpose were what I needed to be satisfied and content inside. - What do you need to be intrinsically satisfied and content and bring wholeness to yourself?

Your Superpower Is Your Story

Stories are important. They preserve history, share experiences and differences, stir up similar memories, make you think beyond what you see, or help you escape. We all love to hear and read stories and have a story to convey. We have become comfortable suppressing our stories because some are too heavy to bear, let alone tell. It's time to understand that sharing your stories breathes oxygen into who you are today and brings about life to your unique story- that life that never ends. As you continue to live, you continue to write your story every day (willingly or unwillingly) and will continue to do so until it becomes your legacy. Our stories are our confirmation of being human- the imperfect being. Our imperfections bring us closer to others and closer to God. Your experiences, accomplishments, hopes, fears, and dreams portray the true you. Your superpower will inspire, empower, uplift, and possibly save that person or people that need it. God chose you as his messenger (a uniquely special role) to bring the message forward. My grandma always said, "Every pot has its cover." Although she was talking about relationships, I saw that it applies here as well. Every story and message sent out has a receiver. Do not deprive your receiver of what is sent to them by God. Use your superpower and tell your story.

Shame was the biggest thing that held me back from telling my story, but then I realized my past or current circumstances do not define who I am today. They are merely milestones on my journey that provided me with the lessons, skills, and experiences I needed to move to the next. I still struggle at times, as we all do, but I take it day by day as I continue my healing journey.

Another word of wisdom my grandma used to say was, "Something is better than nothing." If you're wondering how to start, start small and journal at a comfortable pace: no pressure. If you are not a writer like me, do voice recordings of what comes to your heart and mind. When I decided to begin my storytelling adventure, I hated writing, so I did voice recordings when a piece of my story came to me or something came to my heart and mind. It was easy because I could do it as I was driving or as I lay in bed or walked. You get the picture. Whatever step you decide to take, ponder on this:

- What holds you back from telling your story?
- What do you think you need to overcome that?

The absence of light is represented by darkness, and illumination is the energy of sunlight. In the spiritual realm, it is sometimes defined as awakening or enlightenment. I hope I was able to bring illumination into your life, even if it is just enough to break the darkness, enough to creep into the cracks and crevices we sometimes hide and allow awakening or 'en" light" ment.'

I thank you for receiving my story and helping me continue to heal by allowing me to be vulnerable in this safe space. Remember, God never gives you more than you can handle. You are worthy of the superpowers you have been blessed with, so tell your story, illuminate, and be the light for someone else. Please pay it forward!

ABOUT

THE

AUTHORS

Dr. Barbara Swinney

Dr. Barbara Swinney, Visionary Author, Life and Holistic Leadership Coach, Coach Trainer, Speaker, and Founder and CEO of DEEPER Women™ Lead Global—platform for women in leadership to heal, lead, and LEVERAGE their stories and strategies for life, love, and leadership. Dr. Swinney launched the platform to help women uplevel their life and leadership by offering them the opportunity to LEVERAGE their stories and strategies from the stage at her annual signature event, The DEEPER Women™ Speak Experience. Since the pandemic, more than 100 women have used the DEEPER Women™ Global Platform. Additionally, Dr. Swinney's Ambassador Program, DEEPER Women™ LEVERAGE, provides brand development services to women by helping them increase brand clarity, brand credibility, brand visibility, and expanded impact and influence.

Dr. Swinney launched DEEPER Women™ Lead Global over 5 years ago after journeying through a tumultuous divorce and a major, involuntary shift in her career. She authored the book It's Always *Deeper: Six Steps to Achieving Perpetual Success;* and after much success and thought-provoking discussion during the book tour, she decided to launch an entire platform to offer women opportunities for deeper conversations about how to heal, lead, and LEVERAGE their stories and strategies for life, love, and leadership; teaching women how to expand their leadership capacity, how to forge ahead in the midst of personal crisis, and how to pursue their dreams. *"It has been a privilege to help women go deeper in their lives, businesses, and in leadership,"'* says Dr. Swinney. *I want to make sure we provide practical strategies for women to grow and truly learn how to effectively lead themselves so that they may effectively lead others."*

DEEPER Women Lead Global Signature Programs, Services, and Events:

DEEPER Women LEVERAGE-Ambassador Program

- Business, Brand, and Platform Development designed to increase brand clarity, brand visibility, establish brand credibility, and influence.
- DEEPER Women Speak-Signature Event
- DEEPER Women Magazine
- DEEPER Conversations with Dr. Barbara Swinney

To learn how to connect with DEEPER Women™ Lead Global visit:

IG: @drbarbaraswinney

FB: @barbaraswinneyinc

Twitter: @drbarbaraswinney

LinkedIn: Dr. Barbara Swinney

Website: deeperwomenleadglobal.org

Phone: 770.525.7455

Lee Davis

Lethia Davis (Lee) holds a Master's Degree in Public Administration, Bachelor's Degree in Business Administration, and is a certified Life

Coach. Her education laid the foundation for a remarkable 25-year career in state and local government and in becoming a successful entrepreneur. Her business, BME (Beautiful Minds Entrepreneurship) provides essential services to teens and low-income adults including training, business consulting, and mentorship. Lee is also the host of a new, up-and-coming talk radio show, self-titled The Truth with Ms. Lee on Unit Tea Radio. Lee is also a motivational speaker. Her speeches touch on a wide range of topics, from self-love and self-discovery to pursuing entrepreneurship dreams. Her passion and experience make her a dynamic figure in both the business and motivational speaking realms, with a strong focus on personal growth and entrepreneurial success.

Connect with Lee Davis:

    IG: @thetruth_w_MsLee

Barbara Bond-Gentry

Barbara Bond-Gentry affectionately known as "Coach Bee, the queen of belief" is a Business Mindset Coach, Speaker, Mentor and Boss!! Above all She is deeply committed to her family and faith. She is married to Pastor Mac H. Gentry II and is the proud mother of four amazing children. As the First Lady of K.E.P.T Outreach Ministries, Coach Bee plays an integral role in leading the women of K.E.P.T and serving her community at large. Born and raised in Flint, Michigan, Coach Bee's roots and experiences have shaped her into the resilient and compassionate leader she is today. She is a dedicated professional with a Bachelor of Science degree in Accounting from Norfolk State University. With over 25 years of experience in non-profit accounting, She has become a seasoned expert in financial management and strategy. Currently serving as the Vice President and CFO of Status Home, Inc., She brings her wealth of knowledge and leadership skills to the organization, driving its financial success and mission fulfillment. In addition to her corporate role, Coach Bee is the CEO and Founder of Coach Bee Enterprises, the home of Boss Factory Academy, where she provides coaching and mentorship to aspiring entrepreneurs and business leaders. Outside of her professional endeavors, Coach Bee is also a passionate advocate for women's empowerment and community development. As the founder of The Ladies of My Sister's Keeper Incorporated, she has created a platform to uplift and support women in their personal and professional journeys. In her spare time, Coach Bee enjoys serving as the Head Coach of Beastmode girls Volleyball Team. She also finds joy in teaching balloon classes and creating Beautiful Events with Beeyond Beelief, Balloons Décor and More Inc where she serves as the Founder, Lead Instructor and Head Designer.

Connect with Barbara Bond-Gentry:

> Website: CoachBeellc.com
> Email: info@coachbeellc.com
> Face Book: Barbaa Bond-Gentry
> Instagram: BarbaraBondGentry

Dr. Rhonda Harris-Thompson

Dr. Rhonda Harris Thompson is a highly respected speaker as well as a

life skills and self-mastery coach. She is the recipient of the prestigious Presidential Lifetime Achievement Award. She earned graduate degrees in counseling psychology and general psychology. For the past fifteen years, she has provided workshops, motivational talks, and course materials for self-mastery and personal development. As a former officer in the U.S. Army, she gained invaluable experience that informs her coaching approach for diverse populations and effective leadership.

Dr. Thompson is dedicated to guiding women towards self-mastery and personal excellence. Her genuine concern for those seeking positive change fosters a supportive and nurturing environment for personal growth. Her extensive experience as a military veteran, military spouse, and college professor affords her a unique set of skills and insight. Dr. Thompson developed a comprehensive self-mastery toolkit that equips clients with coping strategies, an understanding of emotional intelligence, unique leadership styles, and productive relationship-building techniques. Dr. Thompson provides exceptional workshops and talks on the use of soft skills. Her expertise has garnered attention from reputable sources, and she has been featured in publications such as NY Weekly.com, CEOweekly.com, Voices of Canada, Victorious by Design, and Who's Who Among Professional Women, further solidifying her reputation as an influential entrepreneur and empowering figure.

Looking ahead, Dr. Thompson will expand her brand by publishing more books, offering her Elite Power Academy course online, and establishing her brand as a sought-after program for personal growth and empowerment.

Connect with Dr. Rhonda Harris Thompson:

Deidre Miller

My name is Deidre Miller. I am a successful thought leader, author, coach, transformational, motivational speaker, consultant, entrepreneur, and the Founder and CEO, 365ELEVATE LLC. I have  spent 28 years in Corporate America, and 20 of those years in a Management/Leadership capacity. I had to climb my way to the top through motherhood, raising two children, being a wife, and earning three degrees in Business, Finance & Accounting. Oh, let's not forget my PHD in the school of hard knocks. After being in corporate America for so long I realize that women are still undervalued, underpaid, not heard, and always having to fight for a seat at the table. I fully understand the physical, mental, and financial struggles, and sacrifices that come with fighting for a seat at that table. Well, I am here to inspire women to stop fighting for the seat and build your own table. It is my purpose and mission to help women in masses turn the invisible glass ceiling into a step to becoming a better version of themselves and accomplish anything they want with the right mindset and confidence from the kitchen table to boardroom table.

Lesli Odum

Lesli Odum is a Wife, Mother, Speaker, addictions counselor, clinical mental health therapist, whose profound testimony of resilience and

impact on people's lives has made her a beacon of hope and inspiration. Her unwavering dedication to helping others navigate their spiritual and emotional journeys has earned her a well-deserved reputation as a compassionate guide and healer. Lesli founded Full Circle Florida, Inc., in 2014 where their mission is to break the cycle of intergenerational Adverse Childhood Experiences, (ACEs) through Mental Health Education, Advocacy and Training. Where they E.A.T mental health! Lesli also Founded POINT TO PINK, a Minority Women's Mental Health Awareness PUSH! Our platform provides a safe and inclusive space for women to learn, grow and heal. Together, they break down barriers, reduce stigma, and prioritize the mental well-being of minority women everywhere. Lesli is quoted as saying,

"We are the Conversation and the Cure."

Connect with Lesli Odum:

www.pointtopink.com

www.fullcirclefloridamentalhealth.com

Bree Reid

Bree Reid is a renowned fashion model, journalist, and entrepreneur based in Atlanta, Georgia. With a keen eye for

style and a flair for the dramatic, Bree has captivated audiences on the runway and beyond. Throughout her career, she has graced the catwalks of over 100 fashion shows and collaborated with top industry professionals, including designers like Zuhair Murad, Assembly Line, and Laquan Smith.

In addition to her modeling career, Bree is the visionary founder of The BR Academy, a prestigious industry preparatory school dedicated to nurturing and empowering aspiring models and actors. Through her academy, Bree provides invaluable mentorship and guidance to help individuals unlock their full potential and achieve success in the competitive world of fashion and entertainment.

Not content to stay in front of the camera, Bree has also made a name for herself as a talented creative director and fashion journalist. Her creative vision was recently showcased in Harper Bazaar Magazine's 2023 holiday digital campaign, where she brought her unique perspective to life on screen. As a freelance writer for leading fashion publications, Bree has uplifted and celebrated the work of countless models and designers, amplifying their voices and helping them build their brands.

Driven by a deep passion for her craft, Bree is a force to be reckoned with in the industry. Her commitment to excellence, combined with her bold sense of style, has earned her a reputation as a trailblazer and innovator in the world of fashion. As she continues to inspire and uplift those around her, Bree's ultimate goal is to empower individuals to embrace their own unique talents and shine brightly in their own right, reshaping the narrative of what it means to be a success in the world of fashion and beyond.

Dearice Spencer-Shackleford

Dearice Spencer-Shackleford epitomizes resilience, empowerment, and unwavering service—a living testament to the

strength of the human spirit. As a first-generation entrepreneur, Motivational Speaker, Certified Master Life Coach, STC-Expert, Reiki Master, Author, US Marine Corp Widow, and devoted mother of three, her journey is a symphony of triumph over adversity.

Raised in the vibrant streets of Brooklyn, New York, Dearice's life took a poignant turn with the heartbreaking loss of her Father and Husband within just 30 days. In the wake of this profound grief, she founded DeariceSpeaksLifeLLC—a platform dedicated to guiding single women and mothers on transformative healing journeys through motivational speaking.

Her commitment to service extends beyond personal triumphs. Volunteering at the 1st Choice Pregnancy and Resource Center in Texarkana, Texas, Dearice taught toddler parenting classes and completed an 8-week course/healing group titled "Surrendering The Secret," focused on healing the heartbreak of abortion. She also served as a polling judge for Bowie County, ensuring her community's voice was heard in county and national elections.

Dearice's expertise is grounded in academic pursuits. Completing her studies at Texarkana College, she earned a degree in Behavioral Science, driven by an interest in psychology and behavior stemming from her father's psychosis. Furthering her commitment to community, she became a Certified Master Life Coach, specializing in Spiritual Transformations, guiding individuals through holistic healing.

Dearice Spencer-Shackleford's story is an anthem of transformation— a reminder that from adversity blooms resilience, and from pain springs empowerment.

Connect with Dearice Spencer-Shackleford:
Website: DeariceSpeaksLifeLLC@gmail.com
IG: @dearicespeakslifellc

Sandra Tescum

Sandra Tescum was born in Belize, Central America, and raised in California and Brooklyn, New York. She considers her spirituality and family to be most important to her.

With 15 years of expertise in Human Resources and Business, Sandra Tescum is a results-driven leader who has proven success in creating collaborative cultures and implementing change to achieve workforce excellence. She delivers talent engagement strategy, motivation, and retention solutions that help organizations leverage their most valuable assets – their employees. She understands the human factors that impact the performance of individuals, teams, and the entire organization. She is passionate and dedicated to creating robust corporate cultures that promote continuous business growth while empowering and motivating employees to realize their full potential and bring their best and most authentic selves to work.

Although most of her career has been in the non-profit sector, she also has HR and Operations expertise in retail, distribution, housing, and technology. She earned a Master of Science in Organizational Leadership and a Bachelor's Degree in Business Administration with a minor in Human Resources from Brenau University. She has also achieved the designations of PHR (Certified Professional in HR), CFI (Certified Forensic Interviewer), and E-Cornell certifications in DE&I, HR Investigations, HR Analytics, Organizational Design, and Leadership Psychology. Sandra is the mother of three wonderful children and a grand dog. In her spare time, she loves playing tennis, dancing, cooking, and baking with her son.

Connect with Sandra Tescum

SandraTescum@gmail.com

LinkedIn: Sandra Tescum

Facebook: Sandra Tescum

Instagram: @Sandra_Tescum